Interpretive Pedagogies for Higher Education

Also available from Bloomsbury

Analysing Teaching-Learning Interactions in Higher Education, Paul Ashwin

Higher Education and the Public Good, Jon Nixon

International Perspectives on Higher Education, edited by Trevor Kerry

Towards Teaching in Public, Mike Neary, Howard Stevenson and Les Bell

Interpretive Pedagogies for Higher Education

Arendt, Berger, Said, Nussbaum and their Legacies

Jon Nixon

BLOOMSBURY
LONDON • NEW DELHI • NEW YORK • SYDNEY

Bloomsbury T&T Clark
An imprint of Bloomsbury Publishing Plc

50 Bedford Square
London
WC1B 3DP
UK

1385 Broadway
New York
NY 10018
USA

www.bloomsbury.com

First published 2012
Paperback edition first published 2013

British Library Cataloguing-in-Publication Data
A catalogue record for this books is available from the British Library.

ISBN: HB: 978-1-4411-1715-1
PB: 978-1-4725-2327-3
ePDF: 978-1-4411-7099-6
ePUB: 978-1-4411-1265-1

Library of Congress Cataloging-in-Publication Data
Nixon, Jon.
Interpretive pedagogies for higher education: Arendt, Berger, Said, Nussbaum, and their legacies/Jon Nixon.
p. cm.
Includes bibliographical references and index.
ISBN 978-1-4411-1715-1 – ISBN 978-1-4411-7099-6 – ISBN 978-1-4411-1265-1
1. Education, Higher–Aims and objectives. 2. Education, Higher–Philosophy.
3. Arendt, Hannah, 1906–1975. 4. Berger, John. 5. Said, Edward W., 1935–2003.
6. Nussbaum, Martha Craven, 1947–I. Title.
LB2322.2.N595 2012
378.01–dc23

2011042163

Typeset by Deanta Global Publishing Services, Chennai, India
Printed and bound by CPI Group (UK) Ltd, Croydon, CR0 4YY

For Pauline

Contents

Preface

This book is the third and last of a series of books that I have written on the state of higher education at the opening of the twenty first century. *Towards the Virtuous University* focused on the moral bases of academic practice. It argued that the activities of research, scholarship and teaching comprise an ethically coherent practice that achieves continuity through traditions that are institutionally sustained by universities committed to questioning their own ends and purposes. The second book, *Higher Education and the Public Good,* argued that higher education is primarily a public good rather than a private or positional gain. The purpose of education is to contribute to the common good and institutions of higher education should be organized in such a way as to further these public ends and purposes. In both books I argued against the increasing marketization and privatization of higher education and for a system of higher education that faces the challenges of widening participation on a global scale.

In *Interpretive Pedagogies for Higher Education* my subject is immediate and contemporary: the assault on higher education through massive cuts in public expenditure and the impact of those cuts on the student experience of learning, the professional identity of academic workers, and the governance of learning. The legacy of interpretive pedagogy that I evoke is severely at risk through a failure of government and a failure of academic leadership across the higher education sector. I argue that we must begin to build from the base – where all the ladders start – with the primacy of pedagogy: the relationship between teacher and taught, between learner and text, between the knower and the knowing. If we start there – in the ordinary common place of learning – we may begin to rebuild. But we can only do so if we carry forward from the past whatever resources of hope remain.

Part I: Origins (Chapters 1–3) sketches this territory with reference to three overlapping contexts. The prime purpose of these chapters is to reposition pedagogy institutionally, educationally and within the interpretive tradition – to provide new bearings on pedagogy. Chapter 1 focuses on the institutional context and poses the question: how can we place pedagogy at the centre of the university's institutional concerns? Chapter 2 provides a brief sketch of the context of public education and asks: how can we ensure that a system of higher education that aspires to be public in its outreach and accessibility is educational in its pedagogic practice? Chapter 3 explores some of the major themes relating to the context of ideas as framed by the interpretive or hermeneutic tradition and leaves us with a further question: how can the pedagogic resources implicit in that tradition carry forward into future generations?

Part II The Legacy (Chapters 4–7) defines these resources with particular reference to the life and work of four outstanding public educators: Hannah Arendt, John Berger, Edward Said and Martha Nussbaum. The essays that comprise these chapters attempt to distil something of their legacy. The organizing themes of these chapters are, respectively, becoming thoughtful, becoming attentive, becoming worldly and becoming responsive. The notion of becoming is central to the argument: the resources of thoughtfulness, attentiveness, worldliness and responsiveness are, crucially, part of our origins, of what is given to us; but they also constitute a beginning, a perpetual renewal. The central chapters of the book provide us with the bare outlines of a pedagogical inheritance: a legacy that carries with it certain obligations or, at the very least, a sense of what we owe to each other and to future generations.

Part III (Chapters 8–10) relates the themes discussed in the previous four chapters to the broader debate on pedagogy as it relates to the higher education curriculum, the ethics of academic and institutional practice across the higher education sector, and the centrality of relationship in all pedagogic practice. Chapter 8 focuses on the need for a higher education curriculum that recognizes the unpredictability of learning outcomes through the development of a flexible framework that allows for differentiation and a heuristic approach to learning. It places the pedagogic debate within the traditional context of the curriculum. Chapter 9 places that debate within the broader context of the ethics of institutional practice. It focuses specifically on the need for reconceptualizing ethics away from rule-bound systems and towards judgement-based practices that are built on mutual trust rather than bureaucratic accountability. Chapter 10 focuses on relationship as the prime space of pedagogy and on the need to develop pedagogic practices that value difference and divergence and that locate these within the broader context of cosmopolitan learning.

This book does not set out to provide a pedagogic 'programme' or 'method'. Nor does it attempt to define a particular 'kind' of pedagogy. It is based on the assumption that there is a need for human beings to reason together (to deliberate and work towards shared understandings regarding differences and right actions) and to act together (within our collective means and in ways that include diverse and sometimes conflicting interests). A further assumption follows and is central to the argument of the book; namely, that we can only reason together and act together insofar as we renounce totalizing explanations that deny the necessity for further deliberation and collective action. My argument is, in other words, based on assumptions that are both humanistic and secular. The point is – always – to keep the argument going beyond the point of seemingly irreconcilable difference.

The prime purpose of the book is to reframe the debate on pedagogy in higher education within this broader set of assumptions and concerns. Pedagogy inevitably raises questions of an ontological, epistemological and ethical nature. It is shaped, in other words, by how we conceive of human being and becoming, of knowledge and belief, and of what constitutes a well-lived life. At the heart of the book is an attempt to understand how those questions have been addressed within a tradition that values interpretation and by some of those who have lived and worked within that tradition. Because that tradition is humanistic and secular, its legacy continues through its openness to the future and to the world. At a time when higher education is under severe threat from government policies that reveal a breathtaking ignorance of both what is being destroyed and the future consequences of that destruction, the legacy provided by the interpretive tradition is of vital importance.

Jon Nixon
Kendal, Cumbria
September 2011

Acknowledgements

This and my previous two books on higher education – *Towards the Virtuous University* and *Higher Education and the Public Good* – would not have seen the light of day had I not benefitted from some exemplary teachers: Dora Bannister taught me as a schoolboy, at Kirkby Lonsdale Grammar School, how to respect complex texts and live with textual difficulty; Dr John Fleeman, a great bibliographer and specialist on the work of Samuel Johnson, taught me as an undergraduate at the University of Oxford to appreciate the complexity of words and their usage; Professor Harold Rosen at the University of London opened my mind to the wonders of the sociology of language; Professor Jean Rudduck, as my doctoral supervisor at the University of East Anglia, taught me the importance of structure in academic writing; and Professor Stewart Ranson, as the director of an ESRC project (based at the University of Birmingham) to which I was attached as a research fellow, introduced me to frameworks of thinking within the field of social and political theory of which I had hitherto been blissfully ignorant. To all these supremely talented and committed teachers and scholars I owe more than I can say.

I thank the Society of Authors for financial support in completing this work of independent scholarship and for the British Library and its staff for providing invaluable advice and support. Thanks also to Professor Ron Barnett, Dr Bruce Macfarlane and Dr Feng Su for their ongoing collegial support and dialogue. During the completion of this work I have also been in regular conversation with Phil Bamber and our exchanges have helped in the clarification of my ideas on some of the matters discussed in this book. I would also like to thank Alison Baker, the commissioning editor at Continuum, who supported my original proposal and provided helpful and timely advice in the early and late stages of drafting. It is a privilege to work with an independent publishing house that is respectful of its authors and sympathetic to the vagaries and unpredictabilities of authorship. Pauline

Nixon has talked through many of the issues discussed in this book and I am grateful for her wise comments, her eloquent silences, her immense capacity for friendship, and her eye for typographical errors and academic waffle. Without her abiding presence – and 'the sunlight on the garden' – this book would not have been completed.

Part One

Origins

One of the prime purposes of this book is to reframe the professional and public debate on pedagogy as it relates to higher education. The three parts of the book set about this task in different ways, each part building on the previous part. The opening chapters outline a number of contexts within which pedagogy and its contribution to higher education are considered. These chapters highlight the importance of the interpretive tradition in rethinking the parameters of pedagogy within the field of higher education. The central chapters of the book consider the work of four thinkers, each of whom has made a distinctive contribution to interpretive scholarship and to our thinking about the nature of interpretation. The relation between the substantive issues addressed by these thinkers and their distinctive modes of addressing them is a unifying theme across these central chapters. The three final chapters explore some of the epistemological and ethical implications of the argument for academic practitioners. These chapters highlight the extent to which pedagogical concerns permeate the practices and structures of higher education.

The assumption underlying Chapters 1–3 is that pedagogy needs to be considered within a broader frame of reference that includes the purpose of the university, the nature of higher education and the broader tradition of interpretive scholarship. It cannot, in other words, be reduced to – or described in terms of – particular techniques or methods aimed at achieving specific pre-formulated outcomes. Given that much of the professional literature on pedagogy is couched in precisely these terms, the prime task is to find different ways of thinking and talking about pedagogy so as to relocate it within the broader debate on the future of higher education and the role of the university in the twenty-first century. What are the contexts – the institutional contexts, the educational contexts and the contexts of ideas – within which pedagogy might be located? The three following chapters have a direct bearing on that question – on how we might formulate it and how we might begin to respond to it.

So, we are concerned in these opening chapters with the direction of movement – the orientation – of pedagogy within its institutional, educational and hermeneutical contexts of origin. That orientation shifts the focus away from pedagogies of technological rationality that require clearly defined objectives, rational planning and observable outcomes and towards interpretive pedagogies that recognize plurality, incommensurability and contingency as factors that inevitably impact upon human understanding. The unifying themes – made explicit in Chapter 3 – are deliberation or practical reasoning as a mode of human understanding, dialogue as the necessary condition for practical reasoning and the centrality of 'the question'. These themes – as explicated and synthesized within the interpretive tradition carried forward in Gadamer's work (2006) on philosophical hermeneutics – define the parameters of pedagogic practice.

Chapter 1

The Place of Pedagogy

But the university of the day after tomorrow can be a place where these best possibilities of teaching are recovered, and in the end these will demonstrate its essential public place in the democracy to come.

(Paul Standish, 2012, 164)

We begin with an overview of the institutional context of pedagogic practice. That context has to be understood with reference to a history of institutional expansion coupled with long-term underfunding culminating in the financial crisis of 2007–2008. The recovery of the UK from that crisis is both slow and weak, whether measured against past profiles of recession and recovery or against the experience of other countries – a point made month on month by the National Institute of Economic and Social Research in its monthly estimates of gross domestic product (GDP). As a result of the government's response to the crisis, its impact is proving long-term and corrosive. The sustainability and viability of the higher education sector, as a whole, is consequently being put at risk, not only through a continuing reduction in the capacity of its provision, but also because that reduction in capacity inevitably leads to changes in what constitutes the pedagogic core of that provision. The richness and necessary complexity of the pedagogic experience – which is the prime legacy of any system of higher education that aspires to be inclusive and participative – is being trimmed back and simplified. There is a crucial question for all those with responsibility for, or interest in, higher education: how can we place pedagogy at the centre of the university's institutional concerns?

The Cost of Expansion

The post-2008 recession has revealed the ever-widening gap between the welfare dream of the post-World War II settlement and its pragmatic realization in the funding policies over the ensuing period. One of the unavoidable questions facing policy makers over the last fifty years had been how to manage their economies in a period of rapid globalization and technological expansion. Crucial to any viable policy response to this question had been the development of a workforce with the necessary skills and understandings to face the challenges of late capitalism. The expansion of higher education was generally assumed to be a necessary precondition of an upwardly mobile and endlessly affluent society: universities were unwittingly or otherwise taking up position in what has turned out to be an increasingly uneasy place between dream and reality, promise and fulfilment, and consumption and cost.

The expansionist trend had been particularly pronounced in the UK and the US. In the US, for example, 'between 1950 and 2000, the number of degree granting institutions more than doubled, from 1,851 to 4,084 with total enrolment increasing from 2.6 million to 14.8 million students, more than fivefold in the fifty years' (Lazerson, 2010, 14). The Netherlands, too, had seen student numbers rise steadily from approximately 50,000 in 1950 to approximately 500,000 in 2006 (see Ritzen, 2010, 162). Judt (2010, 394) highlights the rapidity of that expansion in post-World War II Europe:

> By the end of the 1960s, one young person in seven in Italy was attending university (compared to one in twenty ten years before). In Belgium, the figure was one in six. In West Germany, where there had been 108,000 students in 1950, there were nearly 400,000 by the end of the Sixties. In France, by 1967, there were as many university students as there had been *lycéen* in 1956. All over Europe, there were vastly more students than ever before.

More recently, other national regions have sought to increase educational opportunity at a bewildering pace: Canada, China, Japan, Russia, Singapore to name but a few. That expansion has had a huge global impact and has not come cheap. 'Its cost, to countries not yet recovered from the slump of the thirties and the destruction of the war,' notes Judt, 'was very considerable.' Responses to the soaring costs varied across regions: Ritzen (2010, 133–156) documents what he terms 'the financial suffocation of European universities', while in the US annual expenditure for higher education went from $2.2 billion in 1950 to $134.6 billion in 1990 (National Center for Education Statistics, 2008, Table 187, quoted in Lazerson, 2010, 14). Where expansion has been matched by expenditure, it has been justified on the grounds that universities provide personal advancement and national competitiveness. For the individual, universities were seen as the necessary route to the old and new professions; and, for the state, they provided the resources necessary for keeping ahead in the global markets.

The crucial policy issue was – and is – how, and on what basis, to fund what was considered to be not only a vital but also an essential expansion of the university sector. Responses to this policy issue invariably involved, on all sides of the political spectrum and across the globe, an emphasis on increased privatization and increased profitability. The economic liberalization that characterized the last two decades of the twentieth century and the early years of the twenty-first century did not in itself signal the fall of the welfare state, notwithstanding the best efforts of many of its economic and political theorists. It did, however, illustrate what Judt (2010, 558) has termed 'a seismic shift in the allocation of resources and initiative from public to private sectors'. The claim that an active state is the necessary condition of economic growth and social improvement – of the good and fair society – had been challenged not only by competing ideologies but also by the beneficiaries of that same growth and improvement. The upwardly mobile, increasingly affluent members of the emergent public – with their heightened expectations and their craving for consumer choice – began to balk at paying for the good and fair society.

We are, as Kaletsky (2010) argues in his analysis of the four ages of capitalism, witnessing 'the birth of a new economy'. What 'capitalism 4.0' (as he calls it) will look like is as yet unclear. The road to economic recovery will by almost all reckonings be hard and long. Kaletsky (2010, 274) does, however, point to a new kind of emergent settlement between public and private interests that will meet 'the simultaneous need for more government and smaller government' and be based on a tough debate about 'the balance of responsibilities between government and private enterprise' (p. 274) – a position not dissimilar to that adopted by Stiglitz (2010, 296) who argues for a balance 'between the market and the state, between individualism and the community, between man and nature, between means and ends'. The fundamentalisms of both the political left and the political right have given way to a less strident and more conciliatory analysis of the economic situation.

Madrick (2010), for example, has highlighted the irrationality of the belief that small government is necessarily good government and that big government is necessarily bad government by showing how within the US that belief has led to stagnant wages, rising health care costs, increasing unemployment, extreme inequality and a devastating credit crisis. Ritzen (2010, 87), too, has warned that 'the strategy to limit and reduce budget deficits by cutting higher education and research budgets could very well induce a downwards spiral in European competitiveness'. He insists that 'the best way to reduce budget deficits and public debt is by increasing higher education and research expenditure as the powerhouses for economic growth'. Both Madrick and Ritzen fully acknowledge the need for the kind of balanced settlement that Kaletsky and Stiglitz argue for.

In the meantime, Larry Elliott (2011), one of the most consistently intelligent analysts of the economic scene, warns of 'a fork in the road':

> History suggests there is no iron law of progress and there have been periods when things have got worse not better. Together, the global imbalances, the manic-depressive behaviours of stock markets, the venality of the financial sector, the growing gulf between rich and poor, the high levels of unemployment, the naked consumerism and the riots are telling us something.

Markets and Consumers

There are, however, serious differences regarding particular policy areas. The funding of higher education is one such policy area that in the UK has attracted fierce controversy. Much of that controversy focuses on the underlying assumptions and possible consequences ensuing from the perceived balance being struck between public and private interests. Commenting on the recent funding priorities of the UK coalition government, McKibbin (2010, 12) argues that cuts in public expenditure have 'nothing to do with the economy'. Their importance, he argues, 'is not economic but political and ideological', their ideological purpose being 'to transform a crisis of the banks into a crisis of the welfare state'. Commenting more generally on social policy across Europe and evoking the spirit of Keynes, Soros (2010, 16), too, argues that to cut back on government spending at a time of increasing unemployment is to 'ignore all the lessons learned from the Great Depression'.

The ends and purposes of higher education are not entirely determined by economic factors, but they are informed and shaped by economic considerations. What began over half a century ago as an egalitarian dream of ever-widening access to educational opportunity, a dream of higher education as an intrinsic component of the public good, had from the start to confront economic reality. That reality is harsher now – and the choices starker – than perhaps at any time in the intervening years. But from the outset, the ethical impulse towards the treasured principle of higher education as a public good entitled to unstinting public support has required, as a necessary condition of its sustainability, some hard economic choices. Our current economic situation – defined as a 'crisis' – has exposed some chronic tensions and indeed contradictions in what we understand to be the future of the university in the twenty-first century. 'Crises', as Harvey (2010, 215) points out, 'are the irrational rationalisers of an irrational system'.

Universities find themselves in a marketplace where the students are consumers purchasing their university experience with a view to gaining a degree in a subject most likely to result in postgraduate employment. Contrary to what we are routinely told by politicians peddling regressive policies, this situation was not unavoidable. It resulted from universities becoming increasingly reliant on semi-private, semi-public modes of funding in the face of what Bok (2003) termed the 'rapid growth of money-making opportunities provided by a more technologically sophisticated, knowledge-based economy' (p. 15). Commenting specifically on the situation of higher education within the US, he argued that 'within a few short decades a brave new world had emerged filled with attractive possibilities for turning specialised knowledge into money' (pp. 13–14). Within the UK, too, this emergent trend towards turning knowledge into money had brought about a fundamental change in the culture of higher education. 'Students', claimed Williams (1995, 177), 'have been metamorphosed from apprentices to customers, and their teachers from master craftsmen to merchants'.

Competition for funds and for student numbers led to institutional stratification and the self-protective groupings of institutions, which lobbied intensively for their market niche. Within this context, institutional 'prestige' has itself become a marketable commodity (see Brown, 2011, 25–31). University rankings have become an increasingly important element within this competitive process. Within the UK, the older universities have almost permanent and undisputed occupancy of the premier league, the post-1992 universities are well represented across the broad span of second league institutions and the bottom league is occupied almost entirely by institutions that have gained university status more recently. (Reay, David and Ball, 2005, 140, and Shumar, 1997, 134, point to a similar situation in the US and Australia, respectively). What we see are levels of institutional sedimentation that provide the bases for structural inequalities that define, restrict and control the horizons of expectation and possibility.

'Since the 1980s', writes Lazerson (2010, 84) in his account of higher education as an expression of the American dream, 'published rankings of colleges and universities have intensified the competition, in ways similar to various consumer reports on the quality of every item that is available for sale'. One consequence of this increased competition, he argues, is that higher education in the US has expanded in a segmented and hierarchical fashion in ways that might well be interpreted as having 'preserved the social structure of inequality [T]he overall effect was to leave the nation as socially divided as in the past' (p. 23). Heller (2007, 48–49) adds telling detail to this line of argument in pointing out 'that 77% of all high income students attended a four-year college, while only 33% of poorer students did. While 62% of the higher-income students went to complete a bachelor's degree, only 21% of their lower-income peers were able to obtain this level of education.'

Ongoing research conducted by the UK Sutton Trust supports the view that institutional differentiation driven by the increasing marketization of higher education has tended to reproduce and reinforce structural inequality. In an analysis covering over one million university student admissions during the period 2002–2006, it documented for the first time the extent to which a few individual schools supply the majority of students to the UK's leading research universities – and with lower academic qualifications (see Sutton Trust, 2008). In so doing, it exposed the extent to which a significant proportion of young people from state schools miss out on the opportunity of attending universities to which their peers, with no better or even lower grades at 'A' level but educated privately, gain admission (see, also, Sutton Trust, 2004). 'The overall conclusion', argues Brown (2011, 34), 'must be that, at the very least, marketization has not assisted with widening access; more probably, and in conjunction with privatization, it has set it back.'

Inequality is perceived as acceptable because it is routinely presented as the inevitable consequence of meritocracy – a term famously coined by Young (1958) 'to illustrate the pernicious consequences of a society stratified according to meritocratic criteria, where material resources and social status were bestowed upon the section of the community who were fortunate enough to possess one particular kind of ability, namely marketable talents' (Jackson and Segal, 2007, 124). The metaphor of the level playing field is often evoked at this point to suggest the equal terms upon which everyone competes within the meritocratic game. What the image of the level playing field conveniently brackets out is the fact that what happens *off* the field may be as important, if not more important, than what happens *on* the field in determining the outcome of the game. 'To pretend', as Hattersley (2004, 12) puts it, 'that, because there is no legal prohibition on such activities, the children of the inner cities are free to go to Eton and that their grandparents are free to enjoy Caribbean cruises is a cruel deception'.

The desirability of choice – as an enhancement of commodity value and as a value in itself – is the defining feature of our consumer society: choice is good. No one would argue with this. The thing chosen has a different kind of value than that which is imposed: famine (the imposed thing) is radically different from fasting (the chosen thing). But the choice is always from a range of options that are chosen. A fair society is a matter not just of choice, but of the choices available – and of the fair distribution of that availability of choice. There is no point in choice when the conditions necessary for choosing are limited by conditions beyond my control. If the available options differ across society according to criteria that are not relevant to the choices being made, then that society is an unfair society: if, for example, my choice of university course is determined by my family's financial resources rather than by the suitability of that course to my needs and aptitudes. That is the point that Hattersley and Young – from within their tradition of social democracy – are making. Choice is not in itself enough.

A Privatized Public

The concerns expressed by Hattersley and Young regarding the limits of meritocracy were inspired, in part at least, by the social democratic ideal of higher education as a public good contributing to a good and fair society and the wherewithal for living a good life: goodness was civic and social and higher education contributed to the common good. However, as Hattersley and Young knew well, goods are not in themselves either public or private. Their designation as one or the other is a matter of history; or, more precisely, a matter of how people choose to make for themselves a history. A private good becomes a public good only through a process whereby the public gains ownership of what was previously under private ownership. Similarly, a public good becomes a private good only through a process whereby the public loses ownership of what was previously under public ownership. In either case, that process constitutes the core of democratic politics: the struggle to define who owns what.

Economists promote a neat definition of 'the public good': products or services of which anyone can consume as much as desired without reducing the amount available for others. Multiple individuals can consume such products or services without diminishing their value and an individual cannot be prevented from consuming them – whether or not the individual pays for them. These text book distinctions hinge on what are referred to as the 'non-rivalry' and 'non-excludability' criteria: public goods are 'non-rivalrous' in the sense that they are accessible to all (without my consumption reducing your consumption) and 'non-excludable' in the sense that we all have access to them (regardless of our ability to pay for the air we breathe).

These over-tidy distinctions – relating to what is and is not designated 'a public good' – mask the ethical issues that are at stake and that constitute the ongoing political struggle. Within that process of struggle, the notion of 'the public' – what constitutes 'the public' – is itself highly contested and historically layered: within an unrestrained monarchy 'the public' is little more than a body of office holders dependent on the Crown for status and courtly prestige; within a republic 'the public' is an expanded 'body politic' of republican citizens endowed with political will and purpose; within a modern post-republican state 'the public' is literate and reasonable, critical in the defence and promotion of its own vested interests, external to the direct exercise of political power and deeply committed to the ideal of individual freedom.

The latter comprises a more or less informed electorate, for whom property, private ownership and the assumption of merit become the prime *raison d'être*: 'my property is my own because I and I alone have sweated my brow to get it; I have autonomy over it and no claim to share it, especially by the state, is legitimate' (Hutton, 2010, 183). This 'modern' construction of 'the public' is, as Hind (2010, 44) puts it, a 'public of private interests' that has produced 'the paradox of modern power, the fact of a secret public'. What holds this public together is its shared commitment to private gain: the public interest becomes an aggregate of private interests. This is a privatized – and a privatizing – public.

Not surprisingly, this 'public of private interests' judges all questions of dispensability and indispensability according to the criterion of private interest. Short-term gain wins over the long-term public good; or, as Moyo (2011, 90) puts it, 'Western society has spent thirty years attracting the best and the brightest into consulting, financial services and banking – but now that these businesses have imploded in the 2008 crisis – what will these people do?' That depends on geopolitical region: many will join the ranks of the unemployed, some may re-train and re-route their careers and some will simply exit. That is O'Toole's (2009, 221) assessment of the fate of the younger generation of Irish citizens:

> They will go. And this will throw Ireland back into the vortex from which it seemed to have escaped once and for all. Ireland was underdeveloped

> for so long because it was trapped in a vicious circle. Underdevelopment led to emigration which stripped out both population and the forces of change, reinforcing underdevelopment. In the mid-1990s, this vicious circle turned into a virtuous one: a rising economy attracted back emigrants, who in turn boosted the economy. If this process is reversed, Ireland could be facing much more than a decade of austerity.

Higher education is implicated in this global melt down and must take some responsibility for, and learn from, the dire consequences attendant upon 'being thrown back into the vortex' – being 'trapped in a vicious circle'. In all aspects of university life – from access, through class size, course provision and pedagogical approach, to student welfare – institutional profitability and private interest become the decisive factors. Money matters because it carries with it prestige and market value: institutions aspire to be top of the university rankings; students and academics aspire to these highly ranked universities; and, not surprisingly, research funds and international recognition flood in. Thus, the 'public of private interests' continually reproduces its own institutional hierarchies.

The impact of the current policy of deficit reduction through cuts in public expenditure to higher education – and an increased reliance on private funding through the marketization of higher education – is double edged. On the one hand, it clearly reduces access to higher education: a reduction, which, given contributory factors such as the rise in student fees and institutional variations across the sector, hits prospective students from disadvantaged backgrounds with the greatest severity. On the other hand, it undoubtedly reduces the quality of higher education provision for the majority of students in the majority of institutions, with the result that those students who rely most heavily on state support have an impoverished experience of higher education: more mass lectures, less one-to-one tuition, fewer opportunities for seminar discussions, shorter courses. Reduction in public funding puts at risk not only the quantity of higher education on offer, but also the quality of higher education overall.

Within the UK, the government's White Paper, issued by the Department for Business Innovation and Skills, reproduces the tired rhetoric of 'market entry' – thereby opening the gate to the privatization of higher education (both through the establishment of new institutions and the increased involvement and possible takeover of existing 'not for profit' institutions). (Department for Business, Innovation and Skills, 2011). These legislative changes are proposed in the interests of developing 'a diverse and responsive sector': 'diverse', in this context, means 'differentiated' – but differentiated in respect not of need but of affordability; similarly, 'responsive' means 'responsive to the market' – with the emphasis on competitive edge. As Peter Wilby (2011) points out, the result will be 'two tiers of unfairness':

> [S]tudents from prosperous homes will get an expensive education, with the taxpayer bearing not only the upfront cost but also the risks that students drop out, fail their degrees, or wind up in a monastic retreat, making it impossible to repay their loans. The poor will get a cheaper version at one of those universities that you have never heard of. Cheaper means larger teaching groups, less contact with academic staff, more ill-paid, part-time and temporary tutors, less well-stocked libraries, more obsolete science and engineering labs.

There is, therefore, as Stefan Collini (2011, 14) makes clear, a need to ensure that those entering universities 'are not cheated of their entitlement to an *education*, not palmed off, in the name of "meeting the needs of employers", with a narrow training that is thought by right-wing policy formers to be "good enough for the likes of them", while the children of the privileged classes continue to attend properly resourced universities that can continue to boast their standing in global league tables'. There is a need, in other words, to resist some of those aspects of the US system that the UK system seems so eager to emulate. For the US Ivy League System, as Howard Hotson (2011) has shown, is in fact less egalitarian and less successful than the UK system once population is taken into account: the most selective universities within the US admit only 3 per cent of their students from the lowest socio-economic quartile (mostly African-American), while admitting 74 per cent from the highest. Moreover, 'market competition in the United States has driven up tuition fees in the private universities and thereby sucked out the resources needed to sustain good public universities' (p. 22). The idea that market forces will simultaneously drive up standards and drive down prices does not bear critical scrutiny. Yet, it remains the assumption underlying the UK government policy on higher education.

The Pedagogicized University

That is the background to Nussbaum's (2010) argument that whatever in higher education is 'not for profit' is now seriously at risk. Since it is precisely the 'not for profit' component of higher education that Nussbaum sees as indispensible in any serious attempt to educate future generations of global citizens for full participation in a mature democracy, then universities are in her view facing an unprecedented crisis: 'curricular content has shifted away from material that focuses on enlivening imagination and training the critical faculties towards material that is directly relevant to test preparation'; a curricular shift that has, she argues, been accompanied by 'an even more baneful shift in pedagogy: away from teaching that seeks to promote questioning and individual responsibility towards force-feeding for good exam results' (pp. 134–135). According to Nussbaum, it is not only the broad curricular framework of higher education that has been put at risk, but also the richness of the student experience of learning. Of course, more is learnt than is taught and the student experience of learning is much more than the experience of being taught. Nevertheless, what one learns and how one learns is conditioned by practices in which teaching – and how teaching is understood – necessarily plays a major part.

Universities have a crucial pedagogical role to play in ensuring that we learn how to build together an interpretable world within a global context where, as Beck (2009, 18–19) puts it, 'henceforth, there are no merely local occurrences': a world in which occurrences necessarily have unforeseen and unforeseeable consequences and outcomes. This interpretive capacity is a necessary condition of our being able to live together in difference: if we do not learn to live together, we shall at best squander our resources and at worst destroy one another and the planet on which we live. What Beck calls 'controlling rationality' – the rationality of the Enlightenment and, indeed, of the university as it has developed since the Enlightenment – cannot be applied 'to the uncertainty of the effects, the side effects and the side effects of the side effects . . . [since] all attempts at rational control give rise to new "irrational", incalculable, unpredictable consequences'. It cannot comprehend the unknowability of a world in which 'there are no merely local occurrences'.

It is not a 'controlling rationality' that is required, but modes of 'reasonableness' and 'practical knowing' that rely upon our capacity for interpretation. These cannot be compartmentalized into some neat pedagogical or curriculum category. Interpretation does, of course, have a privileged place – and a tradition – within the broad curriculum area known as 'the humanities', but it also relates to the whole life of the university: to what the university is and what the university aspires to be. Interpretive pedagogies presuppose pedagogicized universities in which the task of pedagogy is related to the whole experience of student learning, to the identity and development of academic practitioners, to the management and governance of the institution and to the relation between the institution and the higher education sector as a whole. The pedagogicized university is pedagogical all the way through. Its pedagogical ends and purposes define the kind of institution it is and the kind of institution it aspires to be.

Three characteristics, in particular, define the pedagogicized university. The first is the emphasis it places on the quality of relationship. Institutions that define their ends and purposes with reference to teaching and learning take pedagogical and collegial relationships seriously. How 'quality' is defined in this context is, of course, open to question. However, what is non-negotiable in terms of the argument of this book is that the quality of teaching and learning and the quality of the relationships within which teaching and learning take place are complementary. Good teaching and learning take place in the context of relationships that value reciprocity and mutual respect. Neither human relationality nor human understanding would be possible without the existence of the other. In that sense, the pedagogicized university is necessarily *humanist* in orientation. We learn to interpret the world through dialogue and we achieve dialogue through reciprocity and mutuality.

The second characteristic of the pedagogicized university is its recognition of different viewpoints and its commitment to exploring these differences. This point is usually couched in terms of 'academic freedom': the freedom of academics to pursue their own scholarly interests and to speak their scholarly minds without fear or favour. Insofar as freedom is at issue, then it is as relevant to students as to academics. Moreover, my freedom cannot be gained at the expense of your freedom, if the principle of freedom is to be upheld. From this, perspective freedom is less important than the democratic framework within which our various freedoms are recognized, negotiated and expressed. This, of course, is a classic *liberal* (as opposed to libertarian) position and one which the pedagogicized university exists to maintain. We achieve freedom within an agreed discursive framework – an educated polity – that recognizes the freedom of all.

The third characteristic is the worldliness of the pedagogicized university: its openness to new possibilities and horizons; its willingness to entertain new perspectives and emergent ideas; its constant questioning of what is known in the interests of ascertaining what is as yet unknown or only dimly perceived. The good pedagogical relationship enables teacher and learner to reach out beyond the boundaries of their 'I/you' relationship into the realm of the third person. In an increasingly globalized world that realm is increasingly rich and varied. It is cosmopolitan: not by choice, but of necessity. All learning is now cosmopolitan learning. The pedagogicized university is deeply *secular* in its worldliness and in its acknowledgement of cosmopolitanism as a dimension of human life and human understanding. The pedagogicized university is unconditionally committed to the primacy of the question in confronting the unpredictability and incommensurability of the world.

The humanist, liberal and secular university is not, of course, an atheist university. It does not seek to impose atheist beliefs or to privilege arguments for atheism. On the contrary, the humanist, liberal and secular university is one which protects the right of all to hold their own beliefs – religious, non-religious or anti-religious – and protects the right of believers to practice their religions. It is an institution that recognizes and engages with religious viewpoints and faith positions, but that privileges no one viewpoint or position over another. All viewpoints are subject to the same interpretive scrutiny. While there are, no doubt, faith-based and faith-oriented universities that are tolerant of divergent viewpoints across the faith community and more widely, such institutions are necessarily committed to faith traditions which ultimately privilege dogma over interpretation. The increasing marketization and privatization of higher education will make it increasingly difficult for universities to escape collusion with a variety of vested interests – whether religious or non-religious.

It took one of the greatest – and bravest – of twentieth century theologians to insist on the modern world's 'coming of age' and on the need for faith communities such as his own to embrace 'religionlessness' and to meet secularity on its own terms and on its own rough ground. Dietrich Bonhoeffer, by that time incarcerated in Buchenwald concentration camp and awaiting certain execution, had not 'lost' his faith but refused to privilege it or impose it on others within a prison community of many faiths and none (Schlingensiepen, 2010, 349–356). At stake are the acknowledgement and recognition of radical and unresolved disagreements on issues of value as well as matters of fact: holding the argument open against all the odds until there is at least agreement regarding the fundamental points of disagreement. That is what the 'pedagogicized' university stands for. The intellectual independence of the university is premised on its commitment to humanistic, liberal and secular values.

Therein resides its moral and ethical authority. If, as Ronald Dworkin (2011b, 41) suggests, 'moral standards prescribe how we ought to treat others' and 'ethical standards [prescribe] how we ought to live ourselves', then the university is centrally concerned with how we ought to live our lives with regard to how we treat others. Interpretation is, by this definition, intrinsically ethical, since it is centrally concerned with how we interpret the world in the light of others' interpretations of it. The 'pedagogicized' university, in other words, is not a place of character formation through moral precept or exhortation, but of ethical flourishing through interpretive enquiry and ongoing dialogue. The place of pedagogy is within a thoroughly 'pedagogicized' university that is secular in its institutional affiliation, liberal in its intellectual commitment and humanist in its commitment to the relational dimension of all human learning.

***

The statement that heads this opening chapter draws attention to 'the day after tomorrow', the need for a recovery of the 'best possibilities of teaching', and the necessary relation between those best possibilities and 'the democracy to come'. Paul Standish (2012) reminds us of the importance not only of the practice of teaching and learning, but also of the democratic possibilities and potential inherent in that practice. The privatization and marketization of higher education – and the culture of institutional competitiveness thereby engendered – has displaced pedagogy from its central place within the life of the university and thereby denied those possibilities and that potential. The policy response to the global financial crisis has seriously exacerbated this problem and has put at serious risk many subject areas and courses within the humanities. Even in those areas of the curriculum that are relatively secure, the nature of teaching and learning and the quality of the teaching experience has been deeply affected. We need not only to safeguard pedagogy, but also to prioritize and revitalize it. That can only be done in and through institutions that are thoroughly 'pedagogicized' in their commitment to students as active interpreters of their world. The university must reclaim the practice of pedagogy, but pedagogy must, in turn, shape and inform the ends and purposes of the university.

Chapter 2

Public Education

What characterizes the humanists is a certain faith in education. Since, on the one hand, man is partially undetermined and moreover capable of liberty, and on the other, good and evil exist, one man can become engaged in that process which leads from neutrality to good, and is called education.

(Tzvetan Todorov, 2002, 38)

The previous chapter focused on the changing institutional context of higher education. This chapter relates higher education to conflicting notions of 'public education'. The central theme is the tension between public education operating as a form of social control and reproduction and public education that aspires to be liberating and transformative. This tension is not only between two very different conceptions of education, but also between different conceptions of what constitutes 'the public'. To track the changing conceptions of public education is, therefore, to understand something of the process of democratization – and to locate higher education within that process is to understand how at different times and in different places it inflects towards or away from the ideals of deliberative democracy: are we educating 'the masses' or remaking 'the public'? That, at least since the Enlightenment, has been a crucial question – and remains so as we struggle to develop a 'mass' system of higher education that is responsive to the technological and cultural challenges of the twenty-first century.

Educating 'The Masses'

Although education was not an invention of the age of reason, it was intrinsic to the Enlightenment project. It was, as Zygmunt Bauman (1987) argues in his seminal work *Legislators and Interpreters*, a necessary and constituent element of the 'total effect of designing society according to the voice of

Reason' (p. 69). That voice was clear and unequivocal in its insistence that 'the idea of education stood for the right and the duty of the state to form (best conveyed in the German concept of *Bildung*) its citizens and guide their conduct. It stood for the concept, and the practice, of a managed society' (p. 69). Society required rigorous management because the dominant image of 'the people' remained the one inherited from the absolutist state:

> As an agent, 'the people' had been problematized as an unruly force and seed of rebellion. By the same token, it had been construed as an object for any action aimed at the defence and promotion of social order. Apart from such action, when left to their own resources and allowed to be guided by their own passions, 'the people' had been problematized as the carrier of the most odious, repulsive and socially damaging tendencies – exactly those which the enlightened, rationally organised state set out to extirpate. (p. 77)

The 'masses', it was assumed, required discipline and containment and for that very reason became the objects of tutelage and care: enlightenment was, thus, 'an exercise . . . in extending the powers and the ambitions of the state . . . [and] in the creation of an entirely new, and consciously designed, social mechanism of disciplining action, aimed at regulating and regularizing the socially relevant life of the subjects of the teaching and managing state' (p. 80). The idea of the public educator was central to this task of extending the powers and ambitions of the state into the hearts and the minds of its subjects. The public educator existed to ensure an order – and a precedent – whereby education and enlightenment were clearly distinguished: the multitude was educated into obedient compliance and socially useful occupations in order to provide the social and the economic conditions necessary for the enlightenment of the few. Education and enlightenment were not only at variance. They were at loggerheads in respect of what constitutes 'the public'.

The foundations of this order – and of the powers and ambitions of the state that it sought to maintain – began to crumble with the advent of post-Enlightenment modernity. The three iconic figures of modernity – Freud, Marx and Nietzsche – presented radically different visions of modernity, but agreed that the changes it represented were irreversible and unfinished. Indeed, they were each spokespersons for what they saw as undeniable societal changes that were incomplete, ongoing and open-ended. Central to these changes was the emergence of a new order of intelligentsia, the authority of which was asserted through its radical independence from both state and society. Within this new order, the public educator assumes the mantle of the public intellectual speaking *for* the public and, where and when necessary, *against* state hegemony and societal norms. The public intellectual – independent, intellectually committed, politically engaged – becomes the enlightened representative and guarantor of 'the people' and its educational destiny: the self-conscious, critical and questioning cortex of modernity.

Modernity had always been critical – indeed, self-critical – but *from within*. Self-referential and self-validating, it lacked 'a vantage point which allows the view of modernity itself as an enclosed object, an essentially complete product, an episode of history, with an end as much as a beginning' (p. 117). Once that vantage point had been discovered, the 'taken for granted' assumptions of modernity – 'that the West was superior to the East, white to black, civilized to crude, cultured to uneducated, sane to insane, healthy to sick, man to woman, normal to criminal, more to less, riches to austerity, high productivity to low productivity, high culture to low culture' (p. 120) – were challenged one by one as manifestations of a coherent but flawed structure of power. The old solidarities and subliminal hierarchies gave way to a radical pluralism that required a new ethics of recognition, a new politics of difference and a new kind of intellectual authority.

That authority, insists Bauman, can only be exercised by those who adopt an interpretive stance to the pluralist world. We require 'specialists in translation between cultural traditions' – specialists in 'the art of civilized conversation' (p. 143). Bauman sees the intellectual classes as being the custodians of what, with more than a hint of irony, he proposes as a 'specialism'. The irony lies in the fact that the 'specialism' in question involves crossing intellectual, disciplinary and cultural boundaries; developing new syntheses from apparently disparate traditions; and forming interpretive frameworks within which radical differences of value and belief can be held in critical tension. The 'specialism' that Bauman is proposing would seem to be a kind of generalizing faculty that acknowledges the speciality of its constituent differences. The nurturing and flourishing of this faculty, he argues, will be crucial to the survival of human beings within an increasingly cosmopolitan world.

Although Bauman sees the intellectual as the custodian of this nurturing and flourishing, he does so in terms that highlight its ordinariness, its commonality, its grounding in the vernacular and the demotic: 'to talk to people rather than fight them; to understand them rather than dismiss or annihilate them as mutants; to enhance one's own tradition by drawing freely on experience from other pools, rather than shutting it off from the traffic of ideas' (p.143). To insist on this 'specialism' as a public resource rather than as the preserve of the intellectual classes is to go beyond the limits of Bauman's argument – and to further insist on that resource as a necessary *educational* resource is to go one step further. But it is essential to do so if, rather than excluding 'the people' from an exclusive and excluding Enlightenment, public education is to become the site of a new enlightenment based on 'the art of civilized conversation'. Such a transformation will require a new kind of public educator – for whom the public comprises citizens, not subjects; for whom education is concerned with empowerment, not control; and for whom public education transforms rather than reproduces. In its aspirations towards reaching out and embracing difference, Bauman's proposed 'specialism' implies a radical reconstitution of 'public education' and of what it means to be a 'public educator'.

Nevertheless, the tension between public education conceived as a means of regulation and social control and public education conceived as egalitarian and liberating – or between the enlightenment of the few and enlightenment as a genuinely public resource – remains a defining feature of the cultural politics of the twenty-first century. As we saw in the previous chapter, it continues to play itself out through the institutional disjunctions – between public and private, research-led and teaching-led, old and new, etc – that shape the landscape of the higher education sector. However, that tension can also be felt in the ongoing debate as to what constitutes 'progress' and 'growth' and the part that higher education might play in either or both: 'progress' is often associated with technological advances, but these same advances may (some would argue) have regressive implications and consequences when they become a major priority within higher education; similarly, the emphasis on culture – 'common', 'popular', etc. – may suggest 'growth', but may again (some would argue) have a deleterious impact on higher education when it becomes all-pervasive.

These differences cannot usefully be portrayed as a stand-off between the sciences and the humanities, although that is often how they are misleadingly presented. They denote a more fundamental struggle – and one that cuts across curriculum divides – between competing notions of 'public education' and competing views as to what contribution a 'mass' higher education system has to make to the public good. How we conceive of pedagogic practice within such a system depends to a large extent on how we conceive of 'public education' – and how we conceive of 'public education' depends, in turn, on what we understand by 'the public' and on what kind of a public we want to be a part of. Pedagogy cannot be abstracted from the conditions that shape it and within which it exerts its own shaping influence.

Technology and 'Progress'

The Enlightenment had seen the natural sciences emerge as the principle paradigm for studying the world as object. The natural world held within it universal laws, which once made explicit through the procedures of empirical enquiry could be used to control and manage its affairs. Science held out the promise of an objective and totalizing vision of the natural world: the individual standing objectively in relation to an objectified world. Implicit in this objectifying world view is the notion of the natural world as knowable, controllable and ultimately predictable. Knowledge, control and predictability were central to this scientific paradigm whereby the objectifying distance between subject and object – between the objectified subject and the subject that objectifies – was not only non-negotiable but also incontestable. The maintenance of this distance constituted the supposed scientific 'method' by means of which the supposed scientific 'truth' was discerned.

If the natural world is subject to the universalizing force of objectifying reason, why might not the human world also be similarly objectified? Auguste Comte's hugely influential 1848 *A General View of Positivism* (published in English in 1865) might be seen as a response to precisely this question. The five-volume work presaged the advent of social science and established one of the central tenets of positivism; namely, that authentic knowledge is based on observable facts. Emile Durkheim, born in 1858 the year after Comte's death, later refined and developed positivism as a sociological method. Through seminal works such as *The Division of Labour in Society* (1893), *Suicide* (1897) and *Elementary Forms of Religious Life* (1912) and his founding in 1896 of the journal *L'Année Sociologique*, he established sociology as a major discipline. The scientific method – with its emphasis on empirical and quantifiable data – thus came to dominate not only the natural sciences but also the science of society. The prime task of that method was to maintain a due distance between social scientists and the society that they were seeking to understand. The prime methodological principle was objectivity.

The overriding purpose of the scientific method, however, was that of human control over the complex environment within which we live and plan for the future: in the case of the natural sciences to control the natural world; in the case of the social sciences to control the social world. The scientific method, in other words, was concerned not only with gaining authentic knowledge in the form of observable facts, but also with applying that knowledge in ways that strengthened and extended human control over the given world. Notwithstanding the distinction between 'pure science' and 'applied science', all science aims at producing useful knowledge even if (as in the case of 'pure science') the particular uses cannot be known in advance. Thus, although the scientific method might be distinguished from interpretive modes of enquiry, an element of interpretation is necessarily involved in rendering it applicable within particular circumstances. For all their objectivity scientific 'findings' are useless without the subjectivity of human judgement in the interpretation of their relevance.

The technological 'turn' that science took throughout the various phases of the industrial revolution should be seen, therefore, as intrinsic to the scientific project as originally conceived. The terms 'science' and 'technology' are now linked in ways which are often assumed to be uniquely contemporary. The financial infrastructure that supports scientific enquiry is now almost entirely focused on outcome, impact and applicability as the essential foreground of enquiry and precondition of funding. Research goes hand in hand with development. So-called 'blue skies' research is undertaken, but always on the tacit understanding that the research may yield significant albeit unspecified pay-offs at some later stage. However, this emphasis does not constitute an epistemological break. On the contrary, the 'technological revolution' as we have come to think of it is all of a piece with the founding impulse of scientific enquiry: the impulse, that is, to know the natural and social world and, in knowing it, to control it; and, in controlling it, to enhance its resources and to expand our resourcefulness.

Technology had in effect 'vocationalized' science and in doing so it both 'vocationalized' higher education and 'technologized' it. The turning point within the UK was the mid twentieth century as Europe and the USA emerged from World War II and its economic aftermath. On the afternoon of 7 May 1959, C. P. Snow (Sir Charles, soon to be Lord Snow) delivered the annual Rede Lecture on the theme of 'the two cultures': the 'culture' of the arts and humanities and the 'culture' of the sciences. Snow's (1993) thesis – baldly stated – was that a divide had developed between these two 'cultures' and that what he saw as the regressive forces of the literary culture in particular (those whom he termed the 'natural Luddites') put at risk the onward march of what he termed 'the scientific revolution'. Those located in what he saw as the 'culture' of the sciences had, as he put it, 'the future in their bones' (p. 10) – and that future viewed from the perspective of 1959 Britain was progressive within its own limited terms.

Snow was allying science and technology to what he saw as the necessary democratization of British society. The expansion of higher education which was already underway and that was ratified by the 1963 Robbins

Report gained impetus through Snow's timely and (as it was to prove) highly controversial intervention. Science was now central to public education. The paradigm of the public educator was the applied scientist who could withstand the intense heat of what Harold Wilson in his now famous phrase was to call 'the white heat of technology'. At the core of Snow's analysis (although, as we shall see, some of his adversaries would not grace it with that term) was what he took to be the historic significance of the industrial revolution as experienced in its defining locality and epoch – mid nineteenth century Britain. Its iconic locations – the Lancashire mill towns, the coalmining communities in the valleys of the Rhonda, the steel works of the Don valley, the Nottinghamshire lace factories maintained by piece-work – have become familiar through the endless sentimentalizing of past struggles in the popular media. Snow saw, to his credit, both the potentially progressive import of those struggles and their impact on traditional ways of life: 'by the industrial revolution, I mean the gradual use of machines, the employment of men and women in factories, the change in this country from a population mainly of agricultural labourers to a population mainly engaged in making things in factories and distributing them when they were made' (p. 29). Nevertheless, Snow was unashamedly a reformist and saw in the social and economic upheaval of the industrial revolution the possibility of a better society – the goods of which with careful planning might be more fairly distributed.

It was from that perspective that he saw the need for higher education to expand in the interests of widening access to and participation in higher education. He wanted to move forward on what he saw as a democratizing, progressive, leftward-leaning trajectory, whereby the graduates of the future would be in the vanguard of the technological progress. One of the outcomes of this notion of widening participation based on the need for new forms of technological knowledge appropriate to a rapidly changing economy was that such knowledge became at once more specialized and at the same time more demanding in its inter-disciplinary resourcefulness. This tension between the desire for a 'mass' system of higher education and the need for increased specialization – although unresolved and barely articulated by Snow himself – was of a piece with the desires and the needs of the times. It is hardly surprising, therefore, that, following the Labour Party's election victory in October 1964, Snow accepted Harold Wilson's invitation to join the newly established Ministry of Technology. He took a Life Peerage and until resigning his ministerial post in April 1966 was the government spokesman on technology in the House of Lords. He saw the scientific revolution – advanced through technological innovation – as the motor of democratization and as central to the task of higher education within a forward-looking and progressive society.

Despite Snow's – and, indeed, the Labour government's – attempts to align the technological revolution with the progressive forces of democratization and widening participation, two major concerns lingered: (1) the concern that an expanded system of higher education focusing on the technological needs of society would be seen to be academically second-rate (an updated version of the earlier 'public education' for 'the masses'); (2) a related concern that if science and technology took this route, then the arts and humanities and what remained of the 'pure sciences' would be seen as superior (an up-dated version of the earlier 'enlightenment' for the few). Behind these two concerns lay the question as to whether a 'technologized' system of higher education would genuinely open up educational opportunity or reproduce existing inequalities: would it make for a flatter and more inclusive society or a more hierarchical and exclusive society? Or, more crudely, does 'public' equate to 'polity' or to 'plebeian'? Snow failed to address the first concern and traded quite shamefully on the second concern as a way of avoiding any real engagement with that question.

Culture and 'Growth'

What Snow failed to grasp was the need for a self-critical stance within the scientific tradition for which he claimed to be speaking. For all its robust rhetoric, his championing of that tradition was defensive and dismissive of any alternative viewpoint. Indeed, he famously castigated as Luddites the 'literary intellectuals' who constituted the 'traditional culture' against which he defined his own progressive and forward looking 'scientific culture' (pp. 22–23). Those he termed 'literary intellectuals' were singled out for particular vilification:

> Almost everywhere, though, intellectual persons didn't comprehend what was happening. Certainly the writers didn't. Plenty of them shuddered away, as though the right course of action for a man of feeling was to contract out; some, like Ruskin and William Morris and Thoreau and Emerson and Lawrence, tried various kinds of fancies which were not in effect more than screams of horror. It is hard to think of a writer of high class who really stretched his imaginative sympathy. (pp. 24–25)

Snow is here dismissing writers who had, with sustained intellectual and artistic seriousness, attempted to interpret the impact of the industrial revolution on ordinary lives, on relationships and communities and on culture and society: precisely the effort of 'imaginative sympathy' that Snow was accusing them of having 'shuddered away' from into 'fancies' and 'screams of horror'. Not only that, but Snow as a spokesperson for the 'scientific culture' and – speaking within the precincts of the University of Cambridge that had been examining the National Science Tripos since 1851 – was dismissing as 'traditional' the field of literary studies that had been introduced to that institution as an examinable subject only forty years earlier. The founding in 1919 of the English Faculty at the University of Cambridge had opened up the study of literature beyond the Greek and Latin 'classics' and, in doing so, had opened the university to the possibility of a new public interest in the interpretation of English literature and its place within a common culture.

F.R. Leavis – who at the time of Snow's lecture was a Fellow of Downing College, Cambridge – took three years to respond to Snow and chose to do so in the delivery of the Richmond Lecture at Downing College in 1962. Leavis (1962) began the lecture with an outright attack on Snow's 'tone': 'a tone of which one can say that, while only genius could justify it, one cannot readily think of genius adopting it' (p. 9). While the 'tone' of Snow's lecture is dismissed as 'portentous', its content (Leavis assures us) is 'portentously ignorant'. In particular, it is ignorant of what it means to be fully human: 'of the human history of the Industrial Revolution, of the human significances entailed in that revolution, of literature, of the nature of that kind of collaborative human creativity of which literature is the type, it is hardly an exaggeration to say that Snow exposes complacently a complete ignorance' (p. 10). Snow, we are told at the beginning of only the third paragraph of this lecture, is not only 'not a genius; he is intellectually as undistinguished as it is possible to be' (p. 10). From there on, the *ad hominem* attack intensified and Leavis gave ground on not a single point.

The public response to Leavis's own 'tone' was on the whole negative – partly, perhaps, because those listening to, or reading the text of, Leavis's lecture had forgotten the disparaging and dismissive 'tone' of Snow's original lecture three years earlier. The question remains, however, as to why Leavis chose to adopt – or be overtaken by – a 'tone' which was so personal and vituperative. The obvious answer to that question is that he had to find a way of breaking the mould of the polite discourse within which an occasional lecture of this kind would be normally couched and in so doing ensure that his voice was heard and reported. If that was his intention, then he clearly succeeded.

But Leavis also had something important to say that was in angry defiance of what he saw as the banality of Snow's claims. What was at stake, for Leavis, was the idea of the university. His animus was directed not at science, but at a 'scientific culture' that in its technocratic zeal set itself against the kind of humanistic understanding that he believed lay at the heart of the university. He was questioning the 'two cultures' dichotomy as presented by Snow and was affirming his conviction that 'for the sake of our humanity – our humanness, for the sake of a human future, we must do, with intelligent resolution and with faith, all we can to maintain the full life in the present – and life is growth – of our transmitted culture' (p. 29). 'Growth' – characterized as organic, social and holistic – was set firmly against 'progress' (characterized as mechanistic, materialistic and atomistic).

Snow had set a snare for the likes of Leavis, and Leavis had walked straight into it. His Richmond Lecture seemed to confirm Snow's characterization of 'literary intellectuals' as talking in vague abstractions – 'our humaneness', 'the full life in the present', 'life is growth' – and assuming an air of superior outrage at the very idea of the technicians taking over the academic workplace. Snow had boxed Leavis into a set of false binaries and Leavis had failed to escape that box and argue his case on his own terms. Leavis seemed at the time to have done little more than reassert the problem as defined by Snow and the premises upon which it was based: the 'scientific culture' *versus* the 'traditional culture'; the old literary establishment *versus* the new world of technological enterprise; the cavaliers of the future *versus* the backward looking puritans.

This public exchange did, nevertheless, highlight the extent to which the old binary divides were coming under increasing strain. Both Snow and Leavis foresaw something of the shifting boundaries within the academic territories they were marking out and defending: Snow knew that science was changing rapidly and that with it society was undergoing huge changes; Leavis knew that literature, at its best, was always responsive to those social changes. What neither fully foresaw was how the territories themselves were undergoing structural transformation.

Leavis's influence extended far beyond the confines of his own particular academic territory. His emphasis on the moral necessity of literary judgement was to provide 'new bearings' for a generation of students and scholars across disciplines, as was his insistence on judgement as a 'common pursuit' (Leavis, 1932; 1952). His work inspired ardent devotion among the so called 'Leavisites', but was impossible to ignore even among those who reacted against particular elements within it. Indeed, his work was the one constant in relation to which – and against which – the next generation of post-World War II students had to define their own critical positions and their own agenda for change. Many of them did so by carrying forward the emphasis Leavis had placed on 'our transmitted culture' and imbuing this notion with a new sense of sociological and indeed political import.

Echoes of the distinctive Leavisite idiom can be heard in some of the iconic texts of the post-World War II era: Richard Hoggart's (1957) *The Uses of Literacy: Aspects of Working-Class Life, with Special References to Publications and Entertainments*, Raymond Williams's (1958) *Culture and Society 1780–1950* (followed by his *The Long Revolution* in 1961), E.P. Thompson's (1963) *The Making of the English Working Class.* These books – regularly re-printed and translated – broke new ground in their insistence on culture as 'a whole way of life' that is rooted in the 'common' and the 'ordinary' and that owes as much to political agency as to economic conditioning. They provided the bases from which later generations of academics would go on to develop courses and programmes of study designed to meet the needs and interests of the changing student population.

This body of work and innovative practice gives the lie to Snow's suggestion that 'literary intellectuals' are both Luddites and elitists. However, it does not dispel concerns regarding its vocational relevance and its potential contribution to the economy. These concerns have re-surfaced with a vengeance in the wake of the financial crisis and the policy responses to it. Increasingly, higher education is valued only as a private gain – and even then only when the private gain can be defined in narrowly vocational and economic terms. For those who would wish to broaden the debate, the following questions are highly pertinent: how are we to value growth that does not manifest itself in economic terms? How can higher education be valued as a public good unless it contributes directly to economic growth? How might we value growth in modes of reasoning and understanding the outcomes of which cannot be measured in technological terms? The value in each case is to be found in the value placed in a vibrant public sphere based on the civic participation of an informed citizenry – a value that cannot be measured exclusively in economic terms or framed entirely in terms of vocational outcomes.

Remaking 'The Public'

The technological 'revolution' and the cultural 'turn' have had a profound effect on the form and content of the higher education curriculum: the former in its emphasis on innovation, application and vocationalism within the sciences in particular; the latter in its reorientation of the humanities towards the world of the everyday and commonplace. However, the longer-term effect has been to blur the traditional curriculum divides rather than reinforce them. One of the most striking – and, for some, disturbing – features of higher education is the merging of the technological and the cultural within fields of study that coalesce around the new technologies in the form of, for example, film-, media- and communication-studies courses. Such courses inflect both towards the arts and humanities and towards the applied sciences. These emergent fields of study, while frequently attracting the opprobrium of politicians and conservative academics alike, have redrawn the knowledge map of higher education.

In doing so, they also redefined the constituency of higher education. Expansion of the higher education sector was no longer a question just of access to, but also of participation in, higher education – through the development of courses relevant to the experience and expectations of the expanded studentship. The 'massification' of higher education became a matter of curriculum and pedagogical concern, as well as one of the admission procedures. Higher education was, in effect, creating the conditions necessary for its own sustainability through the development of a curriculum attuned to the particular needs of a hugely expanded and increasingly diversified student intake. The higher education curriculum was becoming comprehensive across the sector as a whole, while becoming increasingly differentiated across institutions. If higher education was being re-shaped by its new and expanded public, that public was itself being remade through its newly acquired access to continuing education.

The technical 'revolution' and the cultural 'turn' were instrumental in re-orientating higher education towards a more extensive public role: a role that connected with a wider public through the common purpose of ensuring that the members of this wider public had the capabilities necessary to contribute to a rapidly changing economy and an increasingly mobile society. At best, then, the 'massification' of higher education was an attempt to ensure that 'the masses' became an educated public. This could be seen as the reverse side of the Enlightenment project: if, as Bauman argued, the Enlightenment excluded 'the masses' by herding them into a form of public education that aimed at discipline and containment, it also held within it the possibility of a form of public education that aimed at self-fulfilment and flourishing. Then – as now – the tension was between, on the one hand, education conceived as social control and the means of reproducing existing hierarchies and inequalities and, on the other hand, education conceived as socially transformative and the means whereby those same hierarchies and inequalities might be challenged and over-turned.

The crucial question is: within which of these two histories should higher education now locate itself? Posing the question in this way emphasizes not only that there is a choice, but also that the choice is part of a centuries-old struggle. Those who favour the reproduction of the *status quo* frequently invoke history and tradition in support of their conservative predilections. It is important to remind ourselves, therefore, that those who seek to challenge the *status quo* and to arrest the reproduction of its inherent inequalities also have their history and their tradition. There is nothing inevitable about the situations we find ourselves in – provided, that is, we view them as socially and historically constructed and, as a consequence, subject to social and historical change.

Tzvetan Todorov (2002) in his intellectual history of the Enlightenment and its legacy – *Imperfect Garden* – explains this struggle in terms of what he calls 'the hidden pact': a pact, that is, between his hypothetical devil and 'Modern Man – Renaissance Man, Enlightenment Man' (p. 2). Humanity, according to this 'hidden pact', would be granted three freedoms: 'the freedom to submit exclusively to his own affections, to his own reason' and the freedom 'to assume the vast domain of his public actions' (p. 2). Humanity was granted supremacy and 'only the political regime chosen by the will of its subjects – now called "democracy" – was judged legitimate'.

However, suggests Todorov, there was a triple price to be paid for liberty – a price which had never been fully stated at the outset: 'the devil hid the price of freedom so that man should develop a taste for it . . . then find himself obliged to clear his debt' (p. 2). Those who grasped the meaning of 'the hidden pact' explained to their contemporaries in the second half of the eighteenth century: 'if you want to keep your liberty, . . . you will have to pay a triple price, first by separating yourself from God, then from your neighbour, and finally from yourself" (p. 3). You will be a materialist ('no more God'); you will be an individualist ('no more neighbour'); finally, you 'will be threatened by dislocation' and 'infinite dispersal' (no more unity of being) (pp. 3–4).

From this 'prophetic' insight, four 'intellectual families' emerged. These families, according to Todorov's philosophical myth, 'still exist in our time, even if overlappings, defections and adaptations have somewhat muddied the picture' (p. 4). The first family – 'the family of conservatives' – were unwilling to pay the price. They acknowledge that the world around them has changed, but 'try to preserve vestiges of it while appealing to the values of the old' (p. 4). The other three families 'are united in accepting and welcoming the advent of modernity' (p. 4). The first of these 'resolutely modern' families comprises 'the proponents of scientism': 'don't worry, they reply, there will be no price to pay because there never was any freedom . . . men are unwittingly led by biological and historical laws, and what they take for their freedom is, more often than not, only their ignorance' (pp. 4–5). The second – 'resolutely modern' – family comprises 'the individualists': 'let man affirm himself in his essential solitude, in his freedom from all moral constraint, in his unlimited dispersal! Let him affirm his will to power, let him serve his own interests' (p. 5).

The final family – the last of the trio embracing modernity – comprises 'the humanists':

> The humanists, the last large family, think, on the contrary, that freedom exists and that it is precious, but at the same time they appreciate the benefit of shared values, life with others, and a self that is held responsible for its actions; they want to continue to enjoy freedom, then, without having to pay the price. The humanists take the devil's threats seriously, but they do not concede that a pact was ever concluded, and they throw down a challenge to him in return. (p. 5)

Part of that challenge – as suggested in the quotation that heads this chapter – was 'a certain faith in education' (p. 38). Given both the indeterminacy of human life and the possibility of human agency, this 'faith' is of paramount importance. Human agency, exercised under the conditions of plurality and indeterminacy, requires as a condition of its fulfilment the capabilities necessary for shared understanding and for mutuality and reciprocity. Insofar as education in general – and higher education in particular – is seen as contributing to this task, it enables us to grow into our freedom without retreating into either the scientific determinism or the individualist isolationism that Todorov warns against. It provides, that is, a public education – an education, the prime purpose of which is not the reproduction of 'the masses' but the remaking of 'the public'.

***

Pedagogy is an educationally purposeful practice and cannot, therefore, be divorced from the educational ends and the purposes that frame it. However, those ends and purposes are themselves shaped by particular notions of 'the good'. Pedagogy is part of what Todorov in the quotation that heads this chapter calls 'that process which leads from neutrality to good'. Pedagogy cannot be value-neutral. In this chapter, I have explored the different value orientations implicit in the notion of 'public education'. The rapid expansion of higher education from a predominantly elite system to a system of restricted but widening access gives particular relevance to the question of how 'public education' should be conceived and valued. The huge technological advances experienced in the post-World War II period, coupled with an opening up of diverse cultural resources of the everyday, gave added urgency to that question – and, crucially, focused it on how understanding might work within, and for, a system of higher education that is seeking to orientate itself towards the public good.

Chapter 3

The Interpretive Tradition

Rather, you have to determine for yourself what you are going to do. And to do this you have to arrive at a comprehension of your situation, reach an understanding with yourself about it. In other words, you have to interpret it!

(Hans-Georg Gadamer, 2001, 79)

So far, I have argued for the centrality of pedagogy within the institutional structures of higher education and for a pedagogy that is inclusive and participative in its orientation, outreach and commitment to public education. In this chapter, I locate pedagogy within the secular and humanistic tradition of interpretation and in so doing define what I consider to be its distinguishing features. Central to my argument is that this tradition is grounded in common – and, indeed, ordinary – modes of understanding. I take my bearings from the work of Hans-Georg Gadamer, who is a pivotal figure in the tradition that I am seeking to sketch. However, readers will, no doubt, take their own bearings. (Alajendro Gonzalez Inarritu, for example, has beautifully captured the import of this tradition in his film trilogy comprising *21 Grams*, *Amores Perros* and *Babel*). This tradition, in its emphasis on interpretation as a process of understanding oneself in relation to one's understanding of others, is highly relevant to a world in which such mutuality of understanding is both an essential and a scarce resource.

The Interpreted World

In mid-eighteenth century Milan, an obscure professor of rhetoric named Giambattista Vico claimed to have uncovered 'the order of all progress from its first origins'. He elaborated this 'order of progress' in terms of what he termed 'the course of nations' central to which was 'the recurrence of human institutions': 'at first there were forests, then cultivated fields and huts, next small houses and villages, thence cities, and at last academies and philosophers' (Vico, 2001, 15). Implicit in his argument is that these human institutions are historically situated, but that they constitute a category that is sustainable across history. Writing both within and against the Enlightenment that had illuminated the scientific potential of the natural world, Vico was exercised by the idea that the divinely ordained natural world can only be understood in the light of the human world that had evolved and was still evolving in time. That world, he sought to show, could only be understood chronologically. Vico set out to establish an understanding of the evolution of human societies that was as revolutionary in its time as Darwin's application of the notion of 'evolution' to the life sciences over a hundred years later. He lay the foundations of what we now categorize as 'the humanities' and of what is now practiced as 'anthropology', 'cultural studies', 'history', 'sociology', etc.

However, the impact of Vico's *New Science* extends beyond 'the humanities'. The third edition of this work published in the year of his death – and 'thoroughly corrected, revised and expanded by the author' – shows how all human knowledge is historically located and therefore open to interpretation. The 'rules' of science, as developed by contemporaries such as Newton, were not – he implied – absolute and for all time. They were necessarily relative to their age and, as such, open to question. They were *interpretable.* Vico routed the tradition of hermeneutic enquiry – that was as old as Socrates – into the modern age of scientific enquiry. He was virtually unrecognized in his day and his work had little influence, but his long-term impact is indisputable. The world is not entirely given, but made through our own understanding of it – and, as Marx went on to argue, if the world is what we make of it, then we can seek to make of it a better world. Vico's great, sprawling and (by our standards) unscholarly work is the hinge upon which the interpretive tradition turns towards historical consciousness.

Two insights, in particular, form the basis of that tradition. The first idea is that all understanding is always already interpretation. In any attempt at interpretation, we are interpreting that which has already been interpreted. The object of our interpretation is a construct that we inherit from the historical layering of countless prior interpretations and re-interpretations. There is no blank page of history upon which we can inscribe our entirely original understandings. History is a palimpsest of layered inscriptions and layered commentaries. The second insight follows from the first. If all understanding is always already interpretation, then the interpreter is always already part of what is being interpreted. The subject that interprets is implicit in the object of interpretation. Notions of 'objectivity' and 'neutrality' as the privileged criteria of rationality become increasingly difficult to justify in the light of this second insight.

These two insights were implicit – rather than explicit – in *New Science*. Vico was feeling his way towards a new world view that was still embryonic. He was fascinated by pre-history and how, prior to a chronological and sequential notion of time, people nevertheless located themselves historically. He understood that the past was another country which had to be understood on its own terms rather than on our terms. His formulation of the 'epochs of world history' into 'the ages of gods, heroes and men' may seem strange and esoteric to us, but in its time it was path breaking in its insistence on past epochs as interpretive constructs expressed in terms of mythology, political constitutions and legal frameworks. History is what we make of it and what we make of it is inextricable from how we understand it. These were the ideas that would inspire and inform the work of Karl Marx and James Joyce. At the time, however, Vico was still finding a language and form within which to express and elaborate them.

A third insight follows from the first two and was developed in particular by Gadamer. If all understanding is always already interpretation and the interpreter is always already part of what is being interpreted, then all understanding necessarily involves an element of self-understanding. Gadamer elaborated this insight with reference to the notion of 'application', which he understood as being implicit in all understanding from the moment of its inception. It is not that understanding is achieved and then applied, but that the application is intrinsic to the process of understanding: 'in all understanding an application occurs, such that the person who is understanding is himself or herself *right there* in the understood meaning. He or she *belongs to* the subject matter that he or she is understanding. Everyone who understands something understands himself or herself in it' (original emphases) (Gadamer, 2001, 47–48). The hermeneutical task, as Gadamer defines it, is to locate oneself within one's own field – or, as he would put it, 'tradition' – of understanding.

The idea of 'tradition' is central to hermeneutics as developed by Gadamer: 'we stand in traditions, whether we know these traditions or not; that is, whether we are conscious of these or are so arrogant as to think we can begin without presuppositions – none of this changes the way traditions are working on us and in our understanding' (ibid, p. 45). Traditions pose questions in response to which we define ourselves and our own sense of purpose. The coherence of any tradition, as understood by Gadamer, can only be defined with reference to its intrinsic plurality and potential for innovation. Traditions are constantly evolving as new generations interpret and re-interpret them and, by so doing, modify and elaborate them. Traditions may initially present themselves to us as assertions, but, as Gadamer (1977, 11–13) insists, 'no assertion is possible that cannot be understood as an answer to a question, and assertions can only be understood in this way. The real power of hermeneutical consciousness is our ability to see what is questionable'.

Central to the argument of Gadamer's (2004) *Truth and Method* is what he calls 'the hermeneutic priority of the question' (pp. 356–371). 'Understanding begins', as he puts it, 'when something addresses us. This is the first condition of hermeneutics' (p. 298). In becoming receptive to that which addresses us, we are opening ourselves to the question it asks of us: 'the essence of the *question* is to open up possibilities and keep them open' (p. 298) (original emphasis). Interpretation is the process whereby we receive the object of interpretation as a question. In clarifying and addressing that question, the interpreter makes plain its meaning. That is why, as Raz (2009, 268) puts it, 'an interpretation states . . . the meaning of the original'. Gadamer's major contribution to the interpretive – or hermeneutic – tradition is his insight into the dialogical nature of all interpretive acts. The inherent structure of that tradition, he argues, is that of question and answer.

The interpretive tradition as understood and developed by Gadamer is not, therefore, a bounded and impermeable system. On the contrary, it is central to the process of practical reasoning – or *phronesis* – whereby we determine what is rational in the specific and concrete situations in which we find ourselves. The notion of *phronesis* is central to this tradition. Gadamer's contribution to the hermeneutical tradition was to insist that *phronesis*, rightly understood, is not simply a process of applying general laws, rules or precepts to specific cases and thereby involving technical knowledge of the means. His central insight was that this process of application necessarily involves – in addition to, and in conjunction with, knowledge of the means – knowledge of the ends. *Phronesis*, in other words, is not just a form of technical reasoning, but a mode of ethical reasoning requiring an understanding of the common good. 'It's clear', as Gadamer (2006, 35) put it towards the end of his life, 'that the knowledge of the means can't leave out of consideration the knowledge of the final end of every action'.

Phronesis is variously translated as 'wisdom', 'reasonableness', or 'practical knowing'. Its prime purpose is 'to bring us to consensus and to mutual understanding' (p. 62). Practical reasoning cannot be reduced to a set of rules or procedures according to which one produces – or reproduces – something.

Nor, insists Gadamer, does it aim at, or provide evidence of, proof: 'phronesis cannot be gauged with a scientific concept like mathematics; it's something quite different' (p. 53). It is not proof that is required, but recognition and reciprocity. *Phronesis* requires us 'to put ourselves in the place of the other, and that means being genuinely considerate of others without desiring to wage war on him' (p. 56).

The overriding significance and continuing relevance of that last statement is evident in a comment made in April 2007 by Abdul Rashid Ghazi. In January of that year, Islamist radicals (including Ghazi) had turned the Red Mosque (Lal Masjid) complex in Islamabad into an armed base and had begun enforcing Shariah law in parts of the capital. In July, security forces stormed the Red Mosque, in a battle in which (according to official figures) 154 people were killed. Ghazi was among those killed by the security forces. However, in the course of the takeover by the radicals, Peter Bergen (of the CNN) and Anatol Lieven (a former journalist working on the London *Times* and specialist on Pakistan) gained access to the Red Mosque complex and conducted an interview with Ghazi. In the course of that interview, Ghazi gave what Lieven terms 'a carefully tailored message to the American people':

> Americans should think and think again about their government's policy. If you talk and try to understand us, you can win our hearts. But if you come to attack us you will never win our hearts and will also never conquer us, because we are very determined people. How much have you spent on this so called war on terror? Trillions of dollars. If you had spent this on helping develop Pakistan and Afghanistan, we would have loved you and never attacked you. (Lieven, 2011, 159)

Phronesis – of which a large part is contained in Ghazi's phrase 'talk and try to understand' – assumes as a defining feature of our humanity the capacity for interpretation. If we live in an already – and always – interpreted world, we cannot simply override the earlier layers of interpretation. Gadamer asserts the universality and commonality of interpretation: interpretation not as a specialized technique or a critical tool for the avoidance of misinterpretation, but as a mode of universal reasoning whereby human beings achieve mutuality and create a shared world. How, together, we interpret the world is fundamental to what the world means and what, individually and collectively, we might and can make of the world. The interpreted world is a world that is amenable to change on the basis of mutual understanding and the possibility of collective action.

The Fusion of Horizons

Gadamer's notion of 'horizon' relates directly to the importance he places in tradition as the legacy of the past to the future and the corresponding debt owed by the present to the past. In *Truth and Method*, Gadamer provides a general explanation of how and why he is using the concept: 'The concept of "horizon" suggests itself because it expresses the superior breadth of vision that the person who is trying to understand must have. To acquire a horizon means that one learns to look beyond what is close at hand – not in order to look away from it but to see it better, within a larger whole and in true proportion' (Gadamer, 2004, 304). The concept as applied by Gadamer invariably relates to our understanding of the past and of how we interpret the past with reference to the sources available to us. Gadamer's central point on this matter is that our horizons of understanding are never static: 'Every historian and philologist must reckon with the fundamental non-definitiveness of the horizon in which his understanding moves. Historical tradition can be understood only as something always in the process of being defined by the course of events' (ibid, 366).

The meaning to be derived from any act of interpretation is always *in between*: between the interpreted and the interpreter, between the object of interpretation and the interpreter as subject, between different historical positions and perspectives. This means that the object of interpretation does not simply surrender its meaning as a form of divine revelation or authorial intention. Notwithstanding its historical roots in biblical exegesis, hermeneutics is in this respect both secular and humanist in its assumption that neither divine authority nor authorial intention provides the final arbiter in any interpretive act. There can be no appeal to a divine purpose that lies outside the historical course of events or to a human will that is immune to the consequences of those events. The *in between* nature of human understanding also means that interpretation is not simply imposed – as imported theory or pre-specified criteria – by the interpreter on the object of interpretation. Although the world is always already interpreted, every act of interpretation is a new beginning occasioning a necessary shift in the interpreter's self-understanding; or, as Dunne (1997, 121) puts it, 'the interpreter's horizon is already being stretched beyond itself, so that it is no longer the same horizon that it was independently of this encounter'.

Because both interpreter and interpreted are located in the process of history – *in medias res* – the horizon of interpretation can never achieve permanent fixity. It changes constantly, just as our visual horizon varies with each step we take: 'horizons are not rigid but mobile; they are in motion because our pre-judgements are constantly put to the test' (Gadamer, 2001, 48). Consequently, each interpretation is both unique and open to reinterpretation. Plurality is a defining feature of the interpretive field. This raises the question of whether interpretations are subject to assessment as right or wrong, correct or incorrect, good or bad. If interpretations differ – sometimes to the point of incommensurability – are all interpretations equally valid? Can we claim that some interpretations are better than others? Or that some are 'good enough' and others not 'good enough'? If so, on what basis can we make such a claim?

Clearly, any response to these questions is likely to depend, to some extent, on the context within which the interpretation is being conducted. As Dworkin (2011a) points out, 'a director or actor who offers a new interpretation of *Hamlet* need not (and better not) claim that his interpretation is the only correct one and that all other approaches to the play are wrong' (p. 125). However, in other situations, such scepticism would seem not only odd but also outrageous: 'imagine a judge sending an accused criminal to jail, perhaps to death, or awarding a huge verdict against a civil defendant, and then conceding in the course of his opinion that other interpretations of the law that would have required contrary decisions are just as valid as his own' (pp. 125–126). Dworkin opts for what he terms 'the value theory' of interpretation whereby the truth or otherwise of an interpretation is judged according to the truth or otherwise of the value placed upon the object of interpretation within its own interpretive tradition. Thus, 'when we interpret any particular object or event . . ., we are also interpreting the practice of interpretation in the genre that we take ourselves to have joined: we interpret that genre by attributing to it what we take to be its proper purpose – the value of what it does and ought to provide. Interpretation is therefore interpretive . . . all the way down' (p. 131).

Raz (2009), another eminent philosopher of law, makes a similar point when he argues that 'we should interpret in ways responsive to the reasons we have for interpreting' (p. 236). We should, in other words, interpret according to that which renders our interpretation purposeful, namely, the value of that which is interpreted. Insofar as we interpret that which within its own interpretive tradition is considered to have value, our interpretations are always laden with the values of that tradition; but, insofar as we bring our own values to bear on the act of interpretation, our interpretations have the potential for generating new fusions and new pluralities of value. This is what Gadamer means by the self-understanding that is intrinsic to all acts of interpretation and the necessary mobility of horizon that constitutes such acts. Interpretations can be assessed only within the evolving traditions of interpretation of which they themselves are a constituent.

We can only 'reconstruct an interpretation', as Dworkin (2011a, 134) puts it, by distinguishing: 'first, a background identification of practice or tradition to which the interpretation belongs . . . ; second, a set of assumptions about the purpose of that practice . . . ; and third, a claim that the proffered interpretation realizes those purposive assumptions better than any alternative understanding'. The radical import of this argument is evident in the interpretation provided by the late Lord Bingham (2010), Britain's former senior Law Lord, of the decision taken by the US, the UK and some other states to invade Iraq in 2003. The basis of Bingham's judgement that the invasion constituted 'a serious violation of international law and the rule of law' (p. 124) can be found in his following summary statement:

> A decision as massive and far-reaching as one to invade and occupy a foreign sovereign state must be based on something very much more solid than a good arguable case. The inescapable truth is that the British government wished and tried to obtain a further Security Council resolution authorizing the use of force, but was unable to do so in the face of international opposition and went ahead without. (p. 126)

Bingham was, in other words, judging the UK Government's interpretation of the UN Security Council Resolutions 678, 687 and 1441 and its subsequent decision to invade Iraq according to the criteria that show a marked resemblance to Dworkin's three key elements: 'background' tradition (international rule of law), the 'purposes' implicit in that tradition (international agreement) and the 'realization' of 'background' and 'purpose' (Security Council resolution). The UK Government's interpretation was flawed, according to Bingham, because it lacked a sense of responsibility towards the interpretive tradition that might have given its interpretation and subsequent actions credibility in the eyes of the public and legitimacy in the eyes of the law.

Gadamer's framing of the hermeneutical tradition may seem limited by its overriding emphasis on our understanding of the past. Implicit in his argument, however, is the assumption that the past is always present in the future and that the future is, in wholly unforeseeable ways, always present in the past. We are all located differentially in history. That is the guiding principle of Gadamer's hermeneutical outlook: we are all located in the complex course of events, but our various locations and timeframes are indeterminate and different. Any recourse to intentionality or conviction as privileged sources of interpretive authority regarding what the object of interpretation means is misguided. The meaning is always *in between.* It is in the ever-shifting fusion of horizons.

The Power of Prejudice

What the interpreter brings to the process of interpretation is vitally important. We understand the world in relation to what we bring to it by way of prior assumptions, preconceptions and prejudices. Gadamer takes Husserl as one of his starting points on this matter:

> The naivete of talk about 'objectivity' which completely ignores experiencing, knowing subjectivity, subjectivity which performs real, concrete achievements, the naivete of the scientist concerned with nature, with the world in general, who is blind to the fact that all the truth that he acquires as objective, and the objective world itself that is the substratum of in his formulas is his own *life construct* that has grown within him is, of course, no longer possible, when *life* comes on the scene. (original emphases) (Husserl quoted in Gadamer, 2004, 241)

This is, perhaps, the single most important lesson to be derived from the interpretive tradition: that the interpreter cannot be effaced from her or his own interpretation, that the interpreter is positioned in her or his own interpretation and that interpretation itself is situated in the interpreter. We understand the world in and through our experience of the world. This perspective, as Gadamer (2004, 271) puts it, 'involves neither "neutrality" with respect to content nor the extinction of one's self, but the foregrounding and appropriation of one's own fore-meanings and prejudices'. If we are an integral part of the world that we are seeking to understand, then we can 'formulate the fundamental epistemological question for a truly historical hermeneutics as follows: what is the ground of the legitimacy of prejudices? What distinguishes legitimate prejudices from the countless others which it is the undeniable task of critical reason to overcome?' (p. 278). Prejudice – our historicity – is where interpretation begins: 'the concept of "prejudice" is where we can start' (p. 273). We bring with us to any attempt at interpretation prior values and assumptions that shape what and how we interpret.

Gadamer insists that this importing of ourselves into the process of understanding is a necessary component of that understanding. However, he also insists that we must be aware of what we are importing. Some of our prejudices may assist understanding, while others may distort or deny understanding. A large part of the hermeneutical task involves self-examination through the sifting of prejudices. To have trust in an interpretation is to trust that the interpreter has undergone this process of self-examination in respect of the values and assumptions that have shaped that interpretation. Similarly, to trust in one's own interpretive capacity is not to have blind faith in one's own convictions, but to trust in one's own commitment to questioning those convictions. Trust is a necessary condition of understanding and understanding is a necessary condition of our being in the world. If we trusted nothing in this world of ours, then it would be a world beyond our understanding – and a world beyond our understanding is no longer our world.

That is why Gadamer (1977, 8) argues that hermeneutics cannot be 'restricted to a technique for avoiding misinterpretation': misinterpretation through the application of inappropriate prejudices is to be avoided, but that avoidance does not in itself constitute understanding. I gain understanding not only by rejecting inappropriate prejudices, but also by using other of my prejudices to connect with what I am seeking to understand. In explicit opposition to the scientific ideal of objectivity devoid of all prejudice, Gadamer insists on the productive power of prejudice. He rejects as alienating the mistrust of the subject – and of 'subjectivity' – that he sees as implicit in that ideal. He argues, instead, for the necessity of trusting to the subject – and to 'subjectivity' – in all understanding. He is telling us that it is alright to bring at least some of our baggage along with us when we seek to understand.

Gadamer is not arguing on behalf of relativism: an ethics of 'anything goes'. Rather, he is arguing for an ethics of deliberation. He is arguing on behalf of mutuality and reciprocity as the conditions necessary for whatever shared understanding is necessary for being together. Understanding implies – and requires as a necessary condition – recognition of both selfhood and difference and of the necessary relation between the two. To seek to understand is to adopt an ethical stance – not a moralistic or moralizing stance, but a stance which affirms the central importance of personhood (of the other and of the self). If our world is shaped by our understanding of it, and if that understanding is conditional upon our meeting of minds, then understanding is nothing if not ethical. There is no such thing as value neutrality for those who seek to understand. Value affiliation is part of what constitutes human understanding. We cannot understand unless we are willing to handle – and sort – the baggage we carry with us.

There is nothing new in the deeply Aristotelian idea that there is a necessary relation between understanding and goodness and that this relation has something to do with how we practice that relation through association and participation. This is the central theme uniting Aristotle's work on ethics, politics and poetics: how to *constitute* ourselves. The originality of Gadamer's contribution to this line of thought lies in its injunction to overcome what he sees as the alienation implicit in the ideal of prejudiceless objectivity through an acknowledgement of the self as a constituent element of human understanding: acknowledge the presence of yourself in your own understanding; recognize the other person's understanding as central to your own understanding; develop your understanding as you would a dialogue. Above all, Gadamer insists, there can be no pre-ordained method that can be pursued as a means to a pre-specified end. That is not how human understanding works.

Beyond Method

At the time when Gadamer was writing, 'method' was in the ascendancy. The idea of 'method' was particularly associated with scientific enquiry, but the idea of there being a pre-ordained methodology of enquiry across disciplines and fields of study held sway. For enquiry to be taken seriously – whether within the natural, human or social sciences – it had to be conducted systematically and in accordance with pre-specified methodological procedures. In its most extreme form this scientific positivism – buttressed by the philosophical presuppositions of logical positivism or logical empiricism as it is sometimes termed – claimed that observational evidence is indispensable for knowledge of the world and that only when supported by such evidence could a belief that such and such is the case actually be the case (i.e. be 'true'). A methodical approach to the selection, gathering and analysis of empirical 'data' – and to the inferential process whereby 'findings' were derived from this approach – was and to a large extent still is the means by which scientific enquiry gained legitimacy and public recognition. 'Method' would enable one to gather and analyse 'data' which would then provide knowledge in the form of 'findings'. This became the dominant paradigm of scientific enquiry and exerted a strong influence on the social sciences generally and on social psychology in particular where it was supported by the presuppositions of behaviourism.

The dominance of this paradigm did not go unchallenged. During 1951–1952, Michael Polanyi (who was born in Vienna and brought up in Budapest and had enjoyed a highly successful academic career as a physical chemist of international renown) delivered the Gifford Lectures at the University of Aberdeen. A revised version of the lectures was published in 1958 under the title *Personal Knowledge: Towards a Post-Critical Philosophy*. Polanyi explicitly rejected the claims of the empiricists on the grounds that we invariably believe more than we can prove and know more than we can say. Positivism, he argued, fails to take into account the element of personal commitment – what he called the 'tacit dimension' – in all human understanding. Knowledge may be passed on within a tradition by non-explicit means, so that articulation always relies to some extent on that which cannot be articulated. Polanyi's quarrel was not with the scientific method as such, but with what he saw as its grave limitations and its failure to acknowledge those limitations. The problem lay in the assumptions that science made regarding its own methodological supremacy. The credibility of this critique was, of course, greatly enhanced by his own significant contribution to scientific knowledge.

At the time Polanyi was writing the philosopher Susanne Langer was developing, albeit from a different perspective and intellectual background, her own critique of empiricism within the broad field of social psychology. Langer's philosophical project was to make feeling the starting point of a philosophy of mind. This was to culminate in her three-volume work entitled *Mind: An Essay on Human Feeling* (Langer, 1967; 1972; 1982). At the outset of this work, she challenged what she saw as the 'idols of the laboratory': 'Physicalism, Methodology, Jargon, Objectivity, Mathematization' (1967, 47). Langer explained what she saw as the relation between the second and the fourth items on her hit list – methodology and objectivity – as follows:

> Another source of idolatry is the cultivation of a prescriptive methodology, which lays down in advance the general lines of procedure – and therewith the lines of thought – to be followed. According to its canons all laboratory procedures must be isolated , controllable, repeatable and above all 'objective' . . . The result is a laboratory exhibit of 'behaviour' that is much more artificial than any instrumentally deformed object , because its deformation is not calculated and discounted as the effect of an instrument. Here, indeed, is a critical spot where haste to become scientific destroys the most valuable material for investigation. (1967, 36–37)

Gadamer's starting point in *Truth and Method* is precisely this 'problem of method' as he terms it (Gadamer, 2004, 3–8). Understanding cannot be reduced to a method, although interpretive methods may contribute to our understanding. Gadamer does not deny that there are methods, but denies that method predetermines truth:

> Of course there are methods and one must learn them and apply them . . . As tools, methods are always good to have. But one must understand where these can be fruitfully used. Methodical sterility is a generally known phenomenon. . . . What does the truly productive researcher do? . . . Applying the method is what the person does who never finds out anything new, who never brings to light an interpretation that has revelatory power. No, it is not their mastery of methods but their hermeneutical imagination that distinguishes truly productive researchers. And what is hermeneutical imagination? It is a sense of the questionableness of something and what this requires of us. (Gadamer, 2004, 41–42)

Implicit in Gadamer's critique of method is the idea that understanding involves self-formation and human flourishing that is open-ended in the extent and scope of its proliferation. The application of method, on the other hand, assumes a notion of rationality that seeks closure and predictability. Human understanding, argues Gadamer, must be true to the nature of humanity: a humanity that is necessarily fragile and vulnerable by virtue of its complex interconnectivities and its uncertain relation to the future. Gadamer saw this as a struggle between the human and the natural sciences, with the latter imposing an inappropriate methodology on the former. But his analysis was such as to reframe the terms of the debate in ideological rather than methodological terms: the scientific method when inappropriately applied to the human world insists upon a particular version of humanity. Moreover, since the natural world is always already an interpreted world, the methodology derived from the natural sciences may be severely limited even when applied within its own traditional domain.

Understanding is always beyond method because it requires a recognition of 'the questionableness of something': a 'questionableness' that carries forward what is understood – by way of tradition and practice – into what is not understood. The growth of understanding is only achieved by reaching out: from knowing into unknowing; from articulacy to inarticulacy; from bewilderment to understanding. Method may help us to locate the misunderstandings implicit in past interpretations, but it cannot in itself take the inferential leap into the new interpretive beginnings that constitute a radical break with their own interpretive origins. Understanding, for Gadamer, is always and necessarily a new beginning.

The interpretive tradition finds its defining purpose in pedagogy. Its legacy is not some kind of 'theory' that is independent of pedagogic 'practice'. The tradition is intrinsically pedagogical in its emphasis on the dialogical nature of understanding. It points us in the direction of – gives us an essential bearing on – understanding conceived as a way of being together. At a time when simply being together cannot be taken for granted – when, that is, plurality and difference seem to present insuperable problems at every level – the interpretive tradition may carry forward into the future some of the necessary resources: not guidelines or *aide-memoires* or any of the usual paraphernalia of the 'teaching and learning' industry, but records of what it means to seek to understand.

***

The three previous chapters have sought to provide some bearings by which to locate pedagogy as a form of educationally purposeful practice. Pedagogy was thus located in relation to the institutional context of higher education, the development of public education within a rapidly expanding system of 'mass' education and the interpretive or hermeneutic tradition of human understanding as developed in particular by Gadamer. The purpose of these chapters was not simply to set the scene, but to reframe pedagogy within a broader set of institutional, educational and hermeneutic concerns. To reframe pedagogy in this way is to resist the compartmentalization and technicization of pedagogy and to reassert its relevance to the whole institution, to the broad history of public education and to the developing tradition of interpretive enquiry. It is within this broader context of ideas and critical practice that the four central chapters of the book are located

Part Two

The Legacy

Chapters 4–7 link the practice of pedagogy to the lives and works of four public educators who have sought to extend and deepen the understanding of others. The assumption underlying this approach is that pedagogic practice cannot be divorced from the educational ends and purposes of those who practice it – it can only be understood in terms of the relation between the actions undertaken by those practitioners and their intentions in undertaking those particular actions. It is that relation that renders pedagogic practice intelligible and that enables us to distinguish, for example, between education and indoctrination or an educational assignment and a form of punishment. Why we do what we do defines what it is we are doing. Viewed in this way, pedagogy cannot be reduced to a method, a set of techniques or competencies, or a framework of targets, outcomes or objectives. It has to be understood in relation to the values and beliefs of practitioners who are themselves located within particular settings and traditions that render those values and beliefs intelligible.

These four chapters approach the subject of pedagogy in the light of this insight; namely, that actions are only intelligible – interpretable – as moments within a narrative sequence that has meaning through the purposes agents give to it. That is not to say that the assigned purposes predetermine the outcomes of the actions, since those actions are located within a multiplicity of interpretable histories. The purposes matter in giving meaning to the actions, rather than in defining their outcomes. If we transpose this insight to the particular case of pedagogic practice, then we can see that the values and beliefs of those involved in that practice are constitutive and foundational. They cannot be abstracted from the practice of pedagogy without pedagogy becoming something fundamentally different, for example a technique, a method, a means to an end. Pedagogy is grounded in the practice of shared understanding. It is how we operate when we seek to become the kinds of people who can live, work and think together in the interests of some shared or common good.

The following four chapters (Chapters 4–8) focus, then, on the life and work of four exemplary interpreters who in very different ways have carried forward the interpretive tradition as discussed in the previous chapter. Each is difficult to compartmentalize within a single field or discipline, genre or form, style or idiom, or even institutional context. Yet in each case whatever is exceptional in the work is also exceptional within the life. They exemplify the interpretive life: life lived – uncompromisingly and unstintingly – as an interpretive engagement with self and others. That is not to argue that their interpretations were always right or even appropriate, but simply to insist that for them the world is an interpreted and interpretable world that through the practice of interpretation can be changed if ever so slightly. They are also exemplary because through their work they each insist that if their own interpretations matter then ours also matter. That is what makes them not just public intellectuals, but public educators: their insistence on interpretation as a practice that defines our collective humanity in a world of incommensurable and sometimes irreconcilable human difference.

Chapter 4

Becoming Thoughtful: Hannah Arendt (1906–1975)

Might the problem of good and evil, our faculty for telling right from wrong, be connected with our faculty of thought?

(Arendt, 1978, I, 5)

The question of whether our faculty for telling right from wrong is connected with our faculty of thought is the one which preoccupied Hannah Arendt throughout her life. It was no mere academic question. It lay at the heart of her deeply complex relationship with Martin Heidegger – the man and his work – and shaped her highly controversial response to the trial of Adolf Eichmann which she reported on for *The New Yorker*. A span of almost fifty years lay between her first meeting with Heidegger at Marburg University in 1924 at the age of eighteen and her delivery of the Gifford Lectures at Aberdeen University in 1973 on 'thinking'. During those fifty years, her work focused on the major moral and political issues of the time: the origins of totalitarianism in a period that had seen the emergence of two totalitarian regimes, the nature of the human condition in a century of unprecedented barbarity and the future of the Jewish people in Europe that had witnessed the Holocaust. Each of these topics was in itself a lifetime's work, but for Arendt they were necessarily interconnected even if their interconnectivities could not be made explicit in a systematic explanatory framework. What connected them, for Arendt, was her sense – part intuition, part conviction, part faith – of the moral necessity of thought.

Arendt and Heidegger

No one can deliver a lecture the way you do, nor did anyone before you. (Letter from Arendt to Heidegger, 26 July, 1974, quoted in Ettinger, 1995, 131)

Hannah Arendt met Martin Heidegger in 1924 when she attended his philosophy classes at the University of Marburg. She was barely eighteen and a German Jewess. He was thirty five, married with two young sons and completing his magnum opus *Being and Time* which was published in Germany in 1927. Heidegger became, in Elzbieta Ettinger's (1995) words, Arendt's 'lover, friend, teacher and protector' (p. 3). Less than ten years later, in 1933, he was appointed to the prestigious and highly influential post of rector of the Albert Ludwig University of Freiberg, joined the Nazi Party in the same year and delivered a Rectorial Address identifying himself with the Nazi Party and publically embracing its ideology. In the same year (the year of the Reichstag fire in Berlin), Arendt was arrested and along with her mother held and questioned by the police for over a week. She fled with her mother to Paris by way of Czechoslovakia and Geneva and began eighteen years as a 'stateless person'.

Arendt broke off the relationship with Heidegger in 1926 and transferred to Heidelberg to complete her study of 'love and St Augustine' with Karl Jaspers (Arendt, 1996). The lifelong influence that Arendt and Heidegger had on each other was, nevertheless, incalculable. 'There is no doubt,' as Ettinger (1995) puts it, 'that assessing their mutual dependency and the importance each had for the other is a key to understanding their lives'. Heidegger, notwithstanding his deeply controlling and seemingly callous behaviour, met in Arendt his emotional nemesis. Their mutual correspondence although erratic and irregular was to continue throughout their lives. Arendt, in her turn, had met in Heidegger a mind against which she was constantly testing her own thinking. Dana Villa (1996), in his acclaimed *Arendt and Heidegger,* sees Arendt 'as appropriating Heidegger in a highly agonistic manner; as twisting, displacing and reinterpreting his thought in ways designed to illuminate a range of exceedingly *un*-Heideggerian issues' (original emphasis) (p. 13). (see, also: Villa, 1999, 61–86; Villa, 2008, 302–337). Following a near fatal heart attack, Arendt visited the aging Heidegger one last time in 1975 prior to her second fatal heart attack in December of that year and his death almost six months later.

How could someone like Heidegger, capable of such purity of abstract thought, also be capable of such impurity of political judgement? Did the problem lie in thinking itself or in the kind of abstract thinking that Heidegger excelled at? How could one glory in Heidegger the thinker while being outraged at Heidegger the Nazi propagandist? Arendt never fully resolved these questions but her response to them focused increasingly on a triad of concepts: 'thought', 'action' and 'judgement'. These concepts had formed the backbone of the 1958 work by which she is best known, *The Human Condition* (Arendt, 1998); and during the final years of her life she was still struggling in her last work, *The Life of the Mind*, to clarify and elaborate the relation between these concepts (Arendt, 1978). That work remained unfinished, with the first two volumes in near final draft form and the third projected volume available only in the embryonic form of earlier lectures delivered by Arendt on Kant's political philosophy. However, Arendt was clear on two points, both of which have a direct bearing on the questions posed by her early encounter with Heidegger.

First, she was clear that action is distinct from thought. In November 1972, Arendt participated in debates and discussions at a conference in Toronto, Canada, that was organized by the Toronto Society for the Study of Social and Political Thought and entitled 'The Work of Hannah Arendt'. In the course of one exchange, Arendt insisted 'that thinking and saying are not the same, and to the extent that I wish to think I have to withdraw from the world. I really believe that you can only act in concert and I really believe that you can only think by yourself' (Hill, 1979, 305). Arendt's statement provoked a strong reaction and one of the participants pressed the matter: 'But to a political theorist and a teacher and a writer of political theory, teaching, or theorizing, *is* acting'. However, Arendt was adamant: 'You know, all the modern philosophers have somewhere in their work a rather apologetic sentence which says, "Thinking is also acting." Oh no, it is not! And to say that is rather dishonest. I mean, let's face the music: it is not the same!' (p. 304). Although, as Eduardo Duarte (2001, 208–211) reports, Arendt's riposte was met with a 'chorus of disapproval' from fellow participants, she insisted on the distinction between thinking alone and acting with others.

Second, she was clear that thought is distinct from theory. Between August 1999 and August 2000, two former students of Arendt (from her 1969 class in 'Politics in the Twentieth Century' at the New School for Social Research in New York) corresponded 'about the way in which she educated us'. The correspondence was subsequently published as 'an epistolary essay', the correspondents being Elizabeth Young-Bruehl (the author of a 1982 biography of Arendt and a 2006 reassessment of her continuing significance) and Jerome Kohn (Director of the Hannah Arendt Center and Archive at New School University) (Young-Bruehl and Kohn, 2001). Thirty years after their experience of being taught by Arendt, Kohn recalls that 'the distinction between theorizing, "thinking," and a theory that can be stated as its outcome seems to me to have been crucial for her' (p. 229). A theory of justice, for example, may forestall thinking about justice: 'Arendt is convinced that it is not knowing what justice is, but rather thinking about justice, culminating in the individual act of judgement, that lets justice appear in the world'. For her, this is what Socrates, the purest of thinkers, taught others by his own example: 'His discussions not only of justice but also of all human excellences ended not in theories but in perplexity (aporia), so that he had to go on thinking about them, becoming more just' (pp. 230–231). In response, Young-Bruehl voiced her agreement: 'I agree with you completely that she had no such thing as a theory of education and that she did not really make theories of anything. But she did have characteristic ways of thinking which involved concepts or distinctions she had clarified' (p. 234).

Later in the correspondence, Kohn picks up on that last point when he characterizes one of Arendt's ways of thinking with reference to her 'making distinctions':

> Faced with useless categories of understanding, Arendt began anew by making distinctions, by the time honoured *distinguo*, which, since Aristotle, has been the hallmark of many great thinkers who have set out to understand what previously had not been understood. A is not B, totalitarianism is not tyranny, force is not power, action is not work, work is not labour, the private is not public; thinking is not willing, willing is not judging, sympathy is not compassion, and compassion is not empathy ('I' am not 'Thou'). (pp. 242–243)

Arendt did not dismiss all theory as 'useless categories of understanding', but maintaining the distinction between theory and thinking enabled her to begin anew as an independent and original thinker against the massive bulk and authority of Heidegger's *Being and Time.* Similarly, in maintaining that action is not thought, Arendt is allowing for the possibility that the mind that produced *Being and Time* – the mind she most revered – might be judged separately from the man who acted in support of a regime she abhorred. While 'the time honoured *distinguo*' enabled Arendt, the thinker, to begin anew, it also allowed her to remain cautiously open to the influence of that very different thinker, Heidegger, to whom at the end of her life she was able to write in a letter dated 26 July 1974: 'No one can deliver a lecture the way you do, nor did anyone before you'.

'No Pillars and Props'

> *. . . a new kind of thinking that needs no pillars and props, no standards and traditions to move freely without crutches over unfamiliar terrain* (Arendt, 1970a, 10)

Richard J. Bernstein (2000, 277) has pointed out that although 'it is commonly believed that Arendt started thinking about thinking only late in her career . . . the truth is that Arendt's concern with thinking always exerted a powerful influence on the character of her own passionate thinking'. Indeed, her understanding of 'thinking' seems to have emerged from, or run parallel to, her thinking about other things. For example, *The Origins of Totalitarianism* (first published in 1951) analyses the two major totalitarian movements of the twentieth century, Nazism and Stalinism, and develops a notion of totalitarianism as one of the total domination such that all possibility of independent thought is completely eradicated: 'Totalitarian movements are mass organizations of atomized, isolated individuals. Compared with all other parties and movements, their most conspicuous external characteristic is their demand for total, unrestricted, unconditional and unalterable loyalty of the individual member' (Arendt, 1973, 323).

The most conspicuous consequence of this 'external characteristic' is the eradication of all independent thought. Both Nazism and Stalinism, she argues, 'naturally resulted in the same state of mind, the same concentrated obedience, undivided by any attempt to understand what one was doing' (ibid, 324). That is what distinguished totalitarian regimes from all other regimes including autocratic regimes. The latter seek to gain absolute political power and outlaw opposition, but only totalitarian regimes seek to dominate every aspect of life: in the words of the toast raised by Stalin on 7 November 1937, the twentieth anniversary of the Bolshevik Revolution: 'We will mercilessly destroy anyone who, by his deeds or his thoughts – yes, his thoughts! – threatens the unity of the socialist state. To the complete destruction of all enemies, themselves and their kin!' (quoted in Hiroaki Kuromiya, 2005, 134; also, Timothy Snyder, 2010, 72). Arendt was one of the first Western intellectuals to grasp the enormity of, not only the totalitarian atrocities perpetrated by Nazism and Stalinism, but also their aspirations to total domination and 'subjection' of mind and body. 'The ideal subject of totalitarian rule', as she put it in the final chapter of *The Origins of Totalitarianism*, 'is not the convinced Nazi or the convinced Communist, but the people for whom the distinction between fact and fiction (i.e. the reality of experience) and the distinction between true and false (i.e. the standards of thought) no longer exist' (Arendt, 1973, 474).

The loss of those crucial distinctions she saw as the prime purpose of 'ideological thinking'. There are, she argued, 'three specifically totalitarian elements that are peculiar to all ideological thinking': 'its claim to total explanation'; its independence from all experience such that 'it cannot learn anything new'; and its ordering of facts 'into an absolutely logical procedure which starts from an axiomatically accepted premise, deducing everything else from it'. It is because such thinking 'proceeds with a consistency that exists nowhere in reality' that it provides one with the preconditions for the unthinkable unreality of systematic totalitarian terror, that is, the murder, between 1933 and 1945, of fourteen million inhabitants of what Timothy Snyder (2010) terms the 'Bloodlands' between central Poland and western Russia. 'Ideological thinking', as Arendt understands it, is in complete opposition to what she most values in thinking: its exploratory, experiential and inductive nature. Once 'ideological argumentation . . . has established its premise, its point of departure, experiences no longer interfere with ideological thinking, nor can it be taught by reality'. Ideology is incapable of, and opposed to, the comprehension of what is new and original in human experience (Arendt, 1973, 470–471).

'What Arendt understood best', argues Tony Judt (2009, 75), 'were the psychological and moral features of what she called totalitarianism'. It was through the ongoing attempt to understand those features that she was also gaining an understanding of what constitutes thinking – an understanding gained, not through the development of a theory of thinking, but through the practice of thinking itself. In 1961, she brought together in a single volume entitled *Between Past and Future* a number of previously published essays under the general subtitle of 'Eight Exercises in Political Thought'. These 'exercises' cover a range of substantive topics, but are also quite explicitly experiments in applying a particular kind of 'essayistic' thinking – undertaken, as she puts it, 'in the hope of clarifying the issues and gaining some assurance in confronting specific questions' (Arendt, 1993, 15).

To some, as Judt (2009, 73) notes, her mode of thinking is little more than 'metaphysical musings upon modernity and its ills unconstrained by any institutional or intellectual discipline and often cavalierly unconcerned with empirical confirmation'; yet, as he also acknowledges, 'her refusal to acknowledge academic norms and conventional categories of explanation . . . is precisely what most appeals to her admirers'. Her critics and admirers both agree that, for better or worse, it is the 'unconstrained' quality of her thinking untrammelled 'by any institutional or intellectual discipline' that distinguishes it – 'no pillars and props' as Arendt herself put it.

The Eichmann Trial

Half a dozen psychiatrists had certified him as 'normal' (Arendt, 2006, 25)

The trial of Adolf Eichmann, which Arendt covered for *The New Yorker* in 1961, put to the public test both her own way of thinking and her views on the significance of thoughtfulness and thoughtlessness. Her book, *Eichmann in Jerusalem: A Report on the Banality of Evil*, was first published in the US in May 1963, and provoked what Amos Elon has described as a 'civil war . . . among intellectuals in the United States and in Europe' (Elon, 2006, vii). Put crudely, the controversy focused on two questions: should supposedly self-evident evil be subject to thoughtfulness – should it not simply be condemned? Should such evil be ascribed to something as innocuous as banal assent – should it not be seen as inhuman? Even four decades and a new millennium later, Seyla Benhabib (2000), a writer sympathetic to Arendt, points to 'an astonishing lack of perspective, balance of judgement and judicious expression' in her report on the trial. She also maintains that 'this book is Hannah Arendt's most intensely Jewish work, in which she identifies herself morally and epistemologically with the Jewish people' (p. 65). (see, also: Benhabib, 2010; Bilsky, 2010; Kristeva, 2001; Maier-Katkin, 2010, 245–293; Villa, 2008, 302–337).

Benhabib argues that 'there are at least three socio-historical narratives in *Eichmann in Jerusalem*, each of which could have been the topic of separate volumes': the arrest, detention and trial of Eichmann; the role of the Jewish Councils in cooperating with the Nazi regime; and the role of the German citizenry during the Nazi regime and the Holocaust. It is the coming together of these narratives, argues Benhabib, that baffled her readers: 'at one level it seemed as if Arendt was accusing her own people and their leaders of being complicitous in the Holocaust while exculpating Eichmann and other Germans through naming their deeds banal' (p. 68). Susan Neiman (2002), in her powerful study of evil in modern thought, argues that Arendt's reference to banality is deeply ironic: 'calling evil banal is a piece of moral rhetoric, a way of defusing the power that makes forbidden fruit attractive. The ironic tone she took toward Eichmann was entirely calculated. To call evil banal is to call it boring. And if it is boring, its appeal will be limited' (p. 302) (see, also, Neiman, 2010).

Neiman here echoes Karl Jaspers, who, in an interview conducted in 1965, recalls:

> When Eichmann reveals himself as this nullity, then she laughs, because this denouement is like a joke. She amuses us that when she read the transcripts of the Eichmann interrogation, she laughed – not once but often – loudly to herself. What does this mean? One can discuss back and forth how, in life itself, laughter and irony can be founded in an extraordinary seriousness. (Jaspers, 1986, 521)

What Arendt was struggling with was not only the sense that Eichmann was 'normal', but also that his 'normality' carried with it no awareness whatsoever of the criminal nature of his acts. 'Alas,' she asserted, 'nobody believed him'. What nobody could believe was that the norms by which Eichmann had operated, and which he had so thoroughly and unquestioningly internalized, were so monstrous:

> Half a dozen psychiatrists had certified him as 'normal' . . . He 'personally' never had anything whatever against Jews; on the contrary, he had plenty of 'private reasons' for not being a Jew hater . . . Alas, nobody believed him . . . They preferred to conclude from occasional lies that he was a liar – and missed the greatest moral and even legal challenge of the whole case. Their case rested on the assumption that the defendant, like all 'normal persons,' must have been aware of the criminal nature of his acts, and Eichmann was indeed normal insofar as he was 'no exception within the Nazi regime.' (Arendt, 2006, 25–26)

It was, concluded Arendt, neither insanity nor evil intent that had resulted in Eichmann's evil doing. Rather, it was his 'inability to *think*' (original emphasis). More specifically, it was his inability to think 'from the standpoint of somebody else'. From his own normative perspective, he was exemplary, and since he could conceive of no alternative perspective he was unable to contemplate his own guilt or to judge his own actions: 'The longer one listened to him, the more obvious it became that his inability to speak was closely connected with an inability to think, namely, to think from the standpoint of somebody else'. He was, added Arendt, 'surrounded by the most reliable of all safeguards against the words and the presence of others, and hence against reality as such' (p. 49). He had, as a good citizen, simply carried out the orders that had been given him: to use his not inconsiderable talent for rational planning in the services of a complex and evidence-based method of state-sponsored genocide.

'Heidegger and Eichmann, it turns out, are linked', argues Dana Villa (1999, 85): 'pure thought and thoughtlessness are two sides of the same phenomenon, the incapacity for judgement'. Between thought and thoughtlessness lies the kind of thinking that interests and activates Arendt. It is more difficult than either because it refuses both the consensual symmetry of pure thought and the determinacy that orders the thoughtless rule of method. It values dissensus and indeterminacy. It acknowledges reality: a reality that necessarily constitutes a plurality of standpoints, positions, other people; and, crucially, a plurality that is historically layered within socially constituted individual identities. Reality is complex and thoughtfulness constitutes our cognisance of that complexity. The alternatives are either the unreality of pure thought or the thoughtless adherence to method. Thinking for Arendt was always practical in the sense of being grounded in what Joseph Dunne (1997) calls 'the inextinguishable condition of *plurality*' (original emphasis).

'Representative Thinking'

> *Thinking, existentially speaking, is a solitary but not a lonely business; solitude is that human situation in which I keep myself company.* (Arendt, 1978, I, 185)

Arendt had already covered some of this conceptual ground in the essay 'Truth and Politics' that was included in the 1961 volume *Between Past and Future* already alluded to. The latter was published in the year that Arendt travelled to Jerusalem to cover the Eichmann trial and reflects many of the concerns – including her concern with the relation between thinking and judging – that preoccupied her at this time. In a frequently quoted passage from that essay, she writes: 'Political thought is representative. I form an opinion by considering a given issue from different viewpoints, by making present to my mind the standpoints of those who are absent; that is, I represent them'. She goes on to argue that this process of representation 'does not blindly adopt the actual views of those who stand somewhere else'. Rather it 'is a question . . . of being and thinking in my own identity where actually I am not'. Finally, she claims that 'the more people's standpoints I have present in my mind while I am pondering a given issue, the better I can imagine how I would feel and think if I were in their place, the stronger will be my capacity for representative thinking and the more valid my final conclusions, my opinions' (Arendt, 1993, 241).

It is as if Arendt were positing a republic of the mind: thinking, she argues, is a process of representation, which involves 'thinking in my own identity where actually I am not', my capacity for which provides a measure of 'my final conclusions, my opinions'. The more enlarged my mentality, the more valid my opinions. In a related essay in the same 1961 volume – 'The Crisis in Culture' – Arendt suggests a continuity between opinions validated through this process of 'representative thinking' and the making of judgements: 'judging is one, if not the most, important activity in which this sharing-the-world-with-others comes to pass' (p. 221). Thoughtfulness – defined as 'thinking in my own identity where actually I am not' – is the prerequisite of rightly attuned judgement. 'For', as Dana Villa (1999, 98) argues, 'it is in the process of judgement captured by the notions of "representative thinking" and "enlarged mentality" that plurality is preserved, opinion redeemed and the deliberative rationality enthroned as the political faculty par excellence. To judge is to engage in rational public dialogue, deliberating with others with whom I must finally come to an agreement and decision'.

In the first series of her Gifford Lectures delivered at Aberdeen University in 1973, just two years prior to her second fatal heart attack, Arendt returned to this theme and again focused specifically on the case of Eichmann to drive home her point. The only notable characteristic she could detect in him, she claimed, 'was something entirely negative: it was not stupidity but *thoughtlessness*'. Eichmann had failed 'to *stop* and think', which, as she disturbingly pointed out, 'is so ordinary an experience in our everyday life'. (original emphases) Given the ordinariness of that experience, the question that 'imposed itself' (her phrase) was: 'Could the activity of thinking as such, the habit of examining whatever happens to come to pass or to attract attention, regardless of results and specific content, could this activity be among the conditions that make men abstain from evil-doing or even actually "condition" them against it?' (Arendt, 1978, I, 4–5). This, for Arendt, was not a rhetorical question (a question masquerading as a statement), but a real, pressing question (a question that relentlessly 'imposed itself'). How could *thoughtfulness,* as Arendt conceived it, be preserved in a world where opinion, ideology and dogma deny its necessary plurality?

Her response to that question took the form of an elaboration of what she terms 'the two-in-one' of human plurality as experienced in the activity of thinking:

> Nothing perhaps indicates more strongly that man exists *essentially* in the plural than that his solitude actualizes his merely being conscious of himself . . . into a duality during the thinking activity. It is this *duality*

> of myself with myself that makes thinking a true activity, in which I am both the one who asks and the one who answers. (original emphasis) (p. 185)

Was this later position adopted by Arendt in her final unfinished work a retreat from the political? Was Arendt saying that in a world that has been torn between totalizing ideologies and irreconcilable pluralisms the only remaining place for 'the thinking activity' is 'the *duality* of myself'? Had she finally disengaged thinking from the body politic and relocated it within the disembodied realm of spectatorship? Was she, at the last, content with the seeming solipsism of being 'both the one who asks and the one who answers'?

Or was she – as she had continued to do throughout her life – seeking a provisional settlement between her uncompromising care for the world and her unflinching recognition of the world's potential for dehumanization and self-alienation? Hannah Arendt's greatest legacy is not whatever provisional settlement she was struggling towards, but her own relentless insistence on the need to work together towards such a settlement. She had no political programme to pit against what she saw as the inhumanity and self-alienation of the world, but she did have a belief in the human and integrative power of thinking to transform the world into our common world. Hers was a vision which kept in its mind's eye both the easy (and, in her view, terrible) ordinariness of doing evil and the extraordinary (but, in her view, necessary) difficulty of being good. Although Arendt understood 'representative thinking' to be a necessary condition for the avoidance of evil, she did not claim for it any privileged relation to right action. She saw in it no redemptive or transcendental purpose that would lead inevitably to a better world.

Thought and Action

> . . . *there is more than a mere distinction between thinking and acting. There exists an inherent tension between these two kinds of activity* . . . (Arendt, 2003, 105)

As we have seen, Arendt always drew a distinction between thinking and acting and did not subscribe to the idea that to think is also a form of action – or indeed a kind of inner action. She acknowledged that thinking is an activity, but insisted on the distinction between activity and action: 'activity and action are not the same. The main distinction lies in that I am only with my own self or the self of another while I am thinking, whereas I am in the company of the many the moment I start to act' (Arendt, 2003, 105–106). The realm of thought is 'the two-in-one'; the sphere of action is 'the many' that constitutes the human condition of plurality. We cannot simply step from the realm of thought to the sphere of action. There is no clear causeway between the two. This is the existentialist nub of Arendt's argument: thinking may bring us to the edge of action, but only agency can empower us to take the leap into action.

Why did Arendt insist upon this distinction? Why, as a highly influential public intellectual, did she not claim for her own political thought the accolade of political action? The answer undoubtedly lies partly in her mistrust of some modes of thinking – and of some great thinkers – and partly in her belief that while thoughtlessness may be a precondition of evil it is also paradoxically a characteristic of selfless action. Also, perhaps, it lies in her own nature. She was a deeply thoughtful person who clearly enjoyed the company of her own 'two-in-one'. She was also, however, sometimes stubborn, impetuous and unpredictable in her actions. She knew intuitively that thinking could take her a long way, but that when 'the chips are down' (one of her favourite phrases) action is required. No matter how much thought precedes action, the act itself is original and marks an entirely new start.

Carol Brightman (1995), who knew Arendt personally and edited the correspondence between Arendt and Mary McCarthy, provides a useful illustration of how thought and action sometimes collided in Arendt's life to produce wholly unpredictable consequences. Arendt and McCarthy went on to become lifelong friends:

> Their friendship, however, had to overcome a hapless remark McCarthy made at a party in New York in 1945. In a conversation about the hostility of French citizens to the Germans occupying Paris, she said she felt sorry for Hitler, who was so absurd as to want the love of his victims. It was pure Mary McCarthyism, a remark calculated to offend pious anti-fascists, not Hannah Arendt. But Arendt was incensed. 'How can you say such a thing in front of me – a victim of Hitler, a person who has been in a concentration camp!' she snapped. McCarthy was unable to make amends. Three years later, after they found themselves in a minority at a meeting to discuss the future of *politics*, Arendt, according to McCarthy, turned to her on the subway platform and said: 'Let's end this nonsense. We think so much alike.' McCarthy apologized for the Hitler remark, and Arendt admitted she had never been in a concentration camp, only an internment camp in France. (Brightman, 1995, x)

Through that one act – and McCarthy's readiness to reach out and acknowledge it – Arendt secured a friendship that proved to be one of the most important relationships in both their lives. However, it might never have happened, given the outcome of the first meeting, and was then only initiated by Arendt's act which seems to have been largely dependent on contingent factors. In *The Human Condition,* Arendt discusses acts of forgiveness and promise as the paradigmatic cases of selfless acts. Both forgiveness and promise presuppose the possibility of undoing an irreversible chain of events: the former holds out the possibility of 'being able to undo what one has done', while the latter is 'the remedy for unpredictability, for the chaotic uncertainty of the future' (Arendt, 1998, 237). Forgiving and promising are acts. Of course, Arendt and McCarthy being thoughtful people would, no doubt, have pondered on the situation during the intervening three years. Their prior thinking may have created in them both a state of readiness for what occurred on the subway platform, but the action was wholly independent of the thinking. It was a leap – from the comparative safety of the 'two-in-one' – into plurality and unpredictability.

Thoughtfulness, then, cannot in itself guarantee right action. It may inform our judgements as to what course of action to take, but action is always an entirely new beginning. Unlike behaviour, action is its own end. 'It is in the nature of beginning', wrote Arendt (1998, 177–178), 'that something new is started which cannot be expected from whatever may have happened before'. The unpredictability of new beginnings lies in the 'already existing web of human relationships', as a result of which 'action almost never achieves its purpose': 'although everybody started his life by inserting himself into the human world through action and speech, nobody is the author or producer of his own life story' (Arendt, 1998, 184). The consequences of action are 'boundless'. 'Because', as Arendt argues, 'the actor always moves among and in relation to other acting beings, he is never merely a "doer" but always and at the same time a "sufferer". To do and to suffer are like opposite sides of the same coin, and the story that an act starts is composed of its consequent deeds and sufferings' (p. 190). As agents, we do not and cannot, fully understand the boundless consequences of our deeds: 'the process of a single deed can quite literally endure throughout time until mankind itself has come to an end' (p. 233).

That is the point of recognition at which, for Arendt, politics begins: the recognition, that is, of the plurality of the world and of the need to act together. In her essay entitled *On Violence,* Arendt argues that 'power corresponds to the human ability not just to act but to act in concert'. Power, she insists, is never the property of an individual: 'it belongs to a group and remains in existence only so long as the group keeps together' (Arendt, 1970b, 44). Power, for Arendt, is a matter of capacity, not coercion: 'power to' rather than 'power over'. Deconstructing the dualism between being powerless and being powerful, Arendt reconstructs power as empowerment: 'power and violence are opposites; where the one rules absolutely, the other is absent. Violence appears where power is in jeopardy, but left to its own course it ends in power's disappearance. Violence can destroy power; it is utterly incapable of creating it' (p. 56). Only action – undertaken together and in concert – can create power – which is why, as Villa (2008, 329) puts it, 'Arendt takes enormous pains to separate the violence that accompanies liberation from oppression from the debate, deliberation and argument that precedes the constitutional creation of a new (legally and institutionally articulated) "space of freedom" [and why] plurality and equality . . . attend even the *ur*-political moment of foundation'.

Arendt's thinking about the relation between thought and action was constantly being revised and developed in response both to her own experience of the world and to events in the world as experienced by herself and others. Thinking and acting never quite settled into a harmonious relation in her understanding of the human condition. Indeed, the inherent tension between thought and action seems to have been a source of much of her intellectual creativity. Just as her own thinking cannot be reduced to a method, so the relation between thought and action cannot be reduced to a system. Her work teaches us, both by example and by its substantive content, that thinking is difficult, that the relation between thinking and acting is complex and indeterminate, and that thoughtfulness alone (notwithstanding its central importance in humanizing the world) cannot provide us with the necessary power to withstand violence and achieve collective agency.

***

Arendt distinguished between abstract-rationalist thought, technical-rationalist thought and the kind of thinking that she herself tried to practice throughout her life. She had respect for the first two forms of thinking, but saw how the one could all too easily be co-opted by totalizing (and totalitarian) ideologies and how the other could all too easily become the technically accomplished means of achieving appalling (and totalitarian) ends. The first saw its awesome apotheosis in Heidegger; the second its banal personification in Eichmann. She never theorized her own mode of thinking as an enlightened alternative to either of these modes of thought. Nor did she attempt to reduce it to a method. Indeed, as she declared in letter to Heinrich Blucher dated 1 August 1941, she harboured an 'old bias against all methodological argument' (Kohler, 2000, 69). She simply went on thinking – 'without pillars and props' and 'from the standpoint of others'. She engaged in public debate throughout her life, but acknowledged that thinking necessarily involves isolation, which she associated not with the experience of loneliness, but with the 'plurality' (a word she insisted upon) of the human condition.

Such thinking cannot be 'taught', but only exemplified, engaged with and absorbed. This has implications for how we conceive of pedagogy. If we are to think of pedagogy from Arendt's angle of vision, then it cannot be restricted to teaching understood as transmission. Pedagogy, from this perspective, is about how we prepare ourselves, and others, for the unpredictability of thinking (without recourse to pre-specified methods and procedures), the making of judgements (the consequences of which, Arendt maintains, are always beyond pre-specification), and for the possibility of action and new beginnings. That is, in part at least, what Jerome Kohn (in Young-Bruehl and Kohn, 2001) means when he writes that 'Arendt never *taught* her own opinions, but she instilled in us the ability to form our own opinions impartially' (original emphasis) (p. 249) and why, perhaps, he came to the conclusion that 'Arendt intended her teaching to be practical' (p. 243) (original emphasis). The pedagogical import of Arendt's work is, as Dana Villa (2001, 20) shows, deeply Socratic in that it 'consists in the endless and seemingly circular questioning of the basic terms of our moral culture, those whose meaning seems self-evident and unarguable. Questioning is an end in itself'.

Chapter 5

Becoming Attentive: John Berger (b.1926)

Hold everything dear

(Berger, 2007a)

John Berger's work is characterized by its attentiveness to the particularities of the world as it appears to us. He draws pictures with words; he invites us to attend to what lies within the frames of those pictures; he asks us to look and, through the activity of looking, to see. His work, as it develops and extends, is increasingly characterized by hospitality, tact and intimacy. For those of us on the left who have grown up with his work, he has been a huge and enduring inspiration. He invites us, in some of his more recent work, to take a journey with him towards events and places that are of the here-and-now, while being out-of-place and out-of-time: 'to the wedding' (1995), to the 'here is where we meet' (2005), 'from A to X' (2008). The space between looking and seeing is a temporal space in which we learn to become attentive: to focus on the thing itself, to place the thing in perspective, to understand its proportions. The culmination of this journey is indeed the holding of everything dear.

Shifting Perspectives

> *The title 'Permanent Red' was never meant to imply that I would not change.* (Berger, 1979, 10)

Berger has become a master of many forms: essay, documentary, film, interview, novel, photographic essay, etc. It is impossible, as yet, to comprehend the entire body of work which is, of course, still in progress. Part of its enduring significance, however, undoubtedly resides in its insistence on transgressing boundaries of genre, style, taste and, crucially, territory. Were we to have come across Berger in the 1950s, however, we would have encountered a young man who had been eighteen when the Labour Party won its iconic victory in the UK General Election and established what has come to be termed the 'post-war settlement': a social democratic consensus the historic achievement of which was the setting up of the Welfare State. That same young man was in his mid twenties in the early 1950s and, as Geoff Dyer (1986, 3) puts it, 'was gaining some notoriety as an art critic'.

That notoriety was given a permanent stamp with the publication, in 1960, of reviews and articles written mainly between 1954 and 1959 and subsequently brought together under the title of *Permanent Red* (Berger, 1979). Berger was nailing his red flag to the people's mast in this collection of occasional reviews and essays. He was clearly reacting against the increasing emphasis on abstraction within the British art scene which was being shaped and promoted both by an older generation of established critics (such as Herbert Read who held some of the most prestigious academic chairs in Fine Arts on both sides of the Atlantic) and by a younger generation of art critics (such as Patrick Heron who, between 1947 and 50, was an art critic for the then highly influential *New Statesman and Nation*).

Many of the new-wave artists, whom both Read and Heron championed – Terry Frost, Barbara Hepworth, Roger Hilton, Ben Nicholson, Naum Gabo, to name but a few – were residents in or around the Cornish coastal town of St Ives. Michael Bird's (2008) *The St Ives Artists* provides a socially nuanced account of this disparate group of artists, sculptors and potters whose artistic preoccupation with abstract form Berger was quite explicitly positioning himself against. Having shifted from Paris and not yet migrated to New York, the art market alighted albeit briefly on the tip of the Cornish peninsula. St Ives, proclaimed Heron, had become the 'most influential centre of Western painting' (quoted in Bird, 2008, 11). For Berger, however, much of the work associated with the St Ives group sacrificed social realism to formal abstraction and, in so doing, became inward-looking and self-referential.

These sharp, uncompromising dichotomies – content versus form; realism versus abstraction – focused Berger politically and, no doubt, sharpened his polemics. They also, however, blunted his critical intelligence. The recourse to dichotomy constrained his capacity for attentiveness. In *Permanent Red,* he divides the art world into 'artists defeated by the difficulties' and 'artists who struggle'. Berger is undoubtedly on the side of the latter, whose work he sees as an attempt to struggle with reality and, crucially, bring about change. Those 'defeated by the difficulties', on the other hand, use their art to escape into various forms of idealization, self-absorption or disintegration. The 'artists who struggle' engage in their struggle 'beyond

Bond Street' and are, as Berger puts it, necessarily committed to 'a revolutionary change in our whole society' (pp. 53–57), while the works of the 'artists defeated by the difficulties' grace the walls of the Royal Academy and find favour at the Biennale.

Berger's insights are always perceptive and his underlying argument is deeply serious. Nevertheless, in his early work, the schema too often gets in the way of the seeing – the dichotomy prevents the possibility of fully appreciating that which has already been assigned a critical category. He dismisses, for example, Barbara Hepworth's *Contrapuntal Forms* – 'roughly a sphere scooped out into a spiral' – as 'empty' without any description or appraisal of the aesthetic import or impact of that perceived 'emptiness'. The distinctive particularity of neither the sculpture nor the artist is acknowledged in Berger's breezy dismissal of 'the basic emptiness of sculpture like Miss Hepworth's' (pp. 75–79). Similarly, he makes no mention of a younger generation of artists such as Terry Frost and John Wells, both assistants to Barbara Hepworth in her St Ives studio, whose recent experiences in World War II and their subsequent struggle to survive as artists undoubtedly qualifies them as 'artists who struggle'.

I make this point in order to emphasize Berger's immense achievement in becoming attentive as a writer and as a public educator. He was not granted attentiveness. It was hard won. In a later preface to that early collection of occasional pieces – *Permanent Red* – Berger acknowledges that on re-reading the book he had the impression that he 'was trapped at the time: trapped in having to express all that I felt or thought in art-critical terms' (p. 7). Writing in retrospect, he affirms the central tenets of that earlier faith – 'an absolute incompatibility between art and private property, or between art and state property' – but acknowledges that he 'would be more tolerant today' (p. 7). However, what he does not acknowledge in this later preface is his failure of attentiveness to the artists whose work he entraps in his own 'art-critical terms'. This is not a failure of tolerance, but a failure of what was to become Berger's single most important contribution as artist and public intellectual: his insistence on the necessity of becoming attentive.

It is important, therefore, to understand this failure in order to appreciate Berger's overall achievement. Becoming attentive involved, for Berger, two important discoveries: first, finding a first person singular 'I' that somehow expressed a first person plural 'we' and, second, finding a genre that would both contain and contest that collective 'I'. The critical essays brought together in *Permanent Red* very often address their readers in terms of phrases such as 'I believe that', 'the fact that', 'I know that'. The 'I' is unmediated, non-negotiable, fixed in self-declaration. It asserts. In making the move from oppositional art critic to documentary novelist, Berger was beginning to re-locate himself within his own writing and, in doing so, was turning increasingly to a particular form of narrative that he was to make his own: one in which the 'I' was mediated, negotiable and the form fluid and permeable. His first three novels – *A Painter of Our Time* (1958), *The Foot of Clive* (1962) and *Corker's Freedom* (1964) – can be seen as representatives of the transitional phase. But it is to his two great contrasting works of fiction – his (1972) novel, *G*, and his (1992) trilogy, *Into Their Labours* – that we shall turn to understand his mature handling of the narrative form.

An Imagined Conversation

> *The garden is full of flowers, large trees, grass banks and a lawn.* (Berger, 1974, ix)

There is, however, an important journey that we need to take with Berger before embarking on that task. (The story of the journey is recounted in Berger's introduction to the English edition of Fischer, 1974, ix–xx). It was July 1972 and the place was the state of Styria in Austria. Berger was visiting his old friend Ernst Fischer, who was to die later that day – just before 10 o'clock in the evening – although neither Berger, Fischer nor Fischer's wife were aware of that fact when they met in the garden of the house where Fischer and his wife were spending the summer in a small village near Graz:

> When I arrived in the morning Ernst was walking in the garden. He was thin and upright. And he trod very lightly, as though his weight, such as it was, was never fully planted on the ground. He wore a wide-brimmed white and grey hat which Lou had recently bought for him. He wore the hat like he wore all his clothes, lightly, elegantly, but without concern. He was fastidious – not about the details of dress, but about the nature of appearances (Berger, 1974, x).

Fischer had been an Austrian journalist, writer and politician. From 1934 to 1969, he was a member and an important figure in the Austrian Communist Party. He was trying to complete the second volume of his autobiography covering the period 1945 to 1955 – a projected sequel to his (1974) *An Opposing Man* – but took time out for a morning walk:

> We went for a walk together, the walk into the forest he would take each morning. I asked him why in the first volume of his memoirs he wrote in several distinctly different styles.

> 'Each style belongs to a different person'.
> 'To a different aspect of yourself?'
> 'No, rather it belongs to a different self' (p. xiv)

After the walk, they drove down to the nearby town of Graz, where Fischer's wife did some shopping: 'Ernst and I installed ourselves in the lounge of an old hotel by the river. It was in this hotel that I had come to see Ernst on my way to Prague in the summer of '68. He had given me addresses, advice, information and summarized for me the historical background to the new events taking place' (p. xv). They talked about the past, about Fischer's love of his wife, about Ovid. Fischer's wife came back from the shops with some cheese and yoghurt. Fischer said to Berger: 'today we have talked for hours about me . . . you don't talk about yourself. Tomorrow we shall talk about you'. But, of course that conversation never took place because that evening Fischer died of a heart attack.

Had the conversation taken place, it may well have touched on Berger's (1965) *Success and Failure of Picasso*, which he had dedicated to Fischer. They might also have talked about the continuing stream of essays that Berger was producing on a range of artistic and literary topics – collected in his (1969) *The Moment of Cubism and Other Essays* and his (1972) *Selected Essays and Articles: The Look of Things*. They might have discussed the work of the Russian sculptor, Ernst Neizvestny, about whom Berger had recently published his (1969) *Art and Revolution: Ernst Neizvestny and the Role of the Artist in the USSR*. Had there been time, they might also have discussed Berger's hugely influential and widely discussed (1972) *Ways of Seeing* which had been published following the success of the BBC television series. There would certainly have been plenty to talk about.

Berger's more recent work that they might have discussed showed a significant shift from the 'art-critical terms' deployed in *Permanent Red*. However that shift of perspective came about it certainly owed a great deal to Fischer. In *The Necessity of Art*, which Fischer had written in the late 1950s and which had been published in translation by Penguin in 1963, Fischer develops a humanist conception of art which Berger found hugely compelling: 'Fischer had lived through the political consequences of his thought; his book appeared to Berger both as a vision of what he could achieve and the immensity of the labours that still lay ahead' (Dyer, 1986, 31). Fischer's later book, *Art against Ideology* (1969), consolidated Fischer as one of the few committed Marxists developing a humanistic critical perspective on Western art.

In *The Necessity of Art*, Fischer devotes a crucial chapter to 'content and form' and within that chapter provides a statement which, for Berger, must have been of particular significance:

> Subject is raised to the status of content only by the artist's attitude, for content is not only *what* is presented but also *how* it is presented, in what context, with what degree of social and individual consciousness. A subject like 'harvest' can be treated as a charming idyll, as a conventional genre picture, as an inhuman ordeal or as the victory of man over nature: everything depends on the artist's view, on whether he speaks as an apologist of the ruling class, a sentimental Sunday tripper, a disgruntled peasant, or a revolutionary socialist (Fischer, 2010, 149).

This perspective on the relation between subject, content and meaning was written well before what might be seen as Berger's big breakthrough project: *Ways of Seeing*. But it neatly encapsulates many of the central themes of that project. It also calls into question some of the assumptions underlying Berger's earlier critical judgements and his attempt to divide the world into, on the one hand, the defeated formalists devoid of content and, on the other hand, the struggling realists battling against abstractionism. To accept Fischer's argument is to acknowledge that the terms in which Berger defended social realism against, and in opposition to, abstract formalism were at least questionable: if the content of a work of art is, as Fischer maintains, the meaning that the artist makes of the subject matter he or she chooses to engage with, then why should that meaning not be expressed in abstract form? There are further questions – highly relevant to Berger's work – regarding what subject matter the artist chooses to engage with and from what position he or she engages with it. But the earlier tight, dichotomous framings no longer hold.

Escaping the Nominal

> *I do not wish to become a prisoner of the nominal, believing that things are what I name them.* (Berger, 1972, 137)

Two outstanding works of fiction mark Berger's mature middle period. They are hugely contrasting works both in form and subject matter, but they both circle around the issues and questions that might have been discussed in that conversation that never took place on the morning after Fischer's death. Both works mediate between narrator and subject matter in order to realize the full social content of the narrative – in order, that is, to be attentive to what the overlapping and inter-weaving stories that comprise the narrative have to tell us. Berger can only do this by acknowledging the plurality contained within the narrative – a plurality of which he himself is a part. In both *G* and *Into their Labours,* the narrative form is constantly straining against linear consequentiality, uniformity of viewpoint, or any sense of reconciliatory closure. Berger is seeking a narrative form that is attentive to the irreducible complexity – the content – of his subject matter.

The novel *G* seemed to come out of nowhere. Nothing in the three novels that had preceded it could have prepared its readers for its protagonist who, having been raised on a secluded English farm in the 1890s and witnessed events in Europe before the Great War, is caught up in a headlong rush of incident and event as he pursues the extremes of both sexual and political freedom. He defies definition – hence his name 'G' – but is a catalyst within the historic events by which he is swept to his violent death. He is at once Don Giovanni and Garibaldi in his urge for emancipation and yet at the same time dissolves into the necessities of circumstance and history. At once epic in proportion, picaresque in incident and 'fictive' in its handling of form, the novel attracted both notoriety and controversy. It nevertheless won the prestigious Booker Prize for fiction, which Berger accepted while famously donating his prize money to the Black Panthers. (The Guardian Fiction Prize and the James Tait Black Memorial Prize followed in swift succession.)

The author regularly breaks into the narrative to explain the readers his own authorial difficulties or dilemmas. The voice in these passages is not that of a constructed persona, but very much Berger's own reflective voice as we hear it in his essays. In one such extended passage, Berger shares with the reader his preoccupation with both 'the uniqueness of each event' and the possibility of 'development':

> Whatever I perceive amazes me by its particularity. The qualities it has in common with other things – leaves, a trunk, branches, if it is a tree; limbs, eyes, hair, if it is a person – appear to me to be superficial. I am deeply struck by the uniqueness of each event. How am I to convey such uniqueness? The obvious way is to establish uniqueness of development. But I have little sense of unfolding time. The relations which I perceive between things – and these often include casual and historical relations – tend to form in my mind a complex synchronic pattern. And so I am forced to use another method to try and place and define events (Berger, 1985, 136–137).

This alternative 'method' involves building the novel through short passages of prose that are isolated from one another by wide spaces on the page and often by theme and focus. These are interspersed with the kind of essayistic commentary or explanation just quoted – and occasionally by rough child-like drawings or quotations. Berger does not provide his readers with what Dyer (1986, 87) calls 'patiently unfolding naturalistic scenes'. He adopts this approach, as he goes on to explain in the passage quoted above, because he is 'search(ing) for co-ordinates extensively in space, rather than consequentially in time' and because (as he puts it): 'one of the ways in which I establish co-ordinates extensively is by likening aspect with aspect, by way of metaphor. I do not wish to become a prisoner of the nominal, believing that things are what I name them' (Berger, 1985, 137).

Edward Said (2000) makes a similar point in an essay that, while focusing primarily on Berger's use of – and writing about – photography, seems equally applicable to the novel *G* and to his fiction more generally: 'the contemporary world is dominated by monopolistic systems of order, all engaged in the extinction of privacy, subjectivity, free choice. According to Berger, this state of affairs is a consequence of the violent conflation of time with History –objective, official, real – that occurred as part of industrialization in the nineteenth century' (p. 150). This 'violent conflation of time with History' now assumes global proportions and impacts with disproportionate force on the most vulnerable peoples and regions of the world – a theme which Berger takes up in his trilogy (1992), *Into their Labours*.

This great trio of novels – *Pig Earth* (1979), *Once in Europa* (1989) and *Lilac and Flag* (1990) – traces the journey of European peasants from mountain to metropolis. The first two volumes are made up of narratives of varying length. Perhaps the most remarkable and widely read of these narratives is a ninety-page story called 'The Three Lives of Lucy Chabrol', in *Pig Earth*, which is set against the traditional life of a mountain village. The second volume, *Once in Europa*, studies the modernization of that life and shows how that modernization impacts on the relations between men and women. The last volume, *Lilac and Flag*, focuses on the lives of the urban exiles who are themselves less than a generation away from their mountain villages. It shows their absorption into petty crime and their attempt to salvage human dignity from the squalor and degradation of their daily lives.

In many ways, this trilogy is completely different from his earlier novel *G* – and yet it is clearly part of the same intellectual project: the point of that project being to find a way of attending to the human subject, as it defines itself objectively within an increasingly incomprehensible world. Berger takes, as his subject, the European peasant, who, as he sees it, falls outside the frame of class analysis. Citizens, he argues, have become 'insulated' – living 'alone in a service limbo':

> By contrast, the peasant is unprotected. Each day a peasant experiences more change more closely than any other class. Some of these changes, like those of the seasons or like the process of ageing and falling energy, are foreseeable; many – like the weather from one day to the next, like a cow choking to death on a potato, like lightning, like rains which come too early or too late, like fog that kills the blossom, like the continually evolving demands of those who exact the surplus, like an epidemic, like locusts – are unpredictable (Berger, 1992, xxiii).

The trilogy as a whole shows, through multiple and interwoven stories, the clash between a traditional peasant culture of survival which 'envisages the future as a sequence of repeated acts for survival' and cultures of progress that 'envisage future expansion . . . because the future offers ever larger hopes' (p. xx–xxi). The peasant is 'unprotected': 'each day a peasant experiences more change more closely than any other class' (p. xxiii). As the uprooted peasants trail their ways across Europe in the second and third volumes of the trilogy we see history – that big ideologically driven 'History' – closing in on them, cutting off their options, rendering them obsolete. In the brave new metropolis, they are without identity, particularity, specificity: 'millions disappear without trace, leaving behind no landmark. In the city the bereaved alone carry their dead in their heads. The only memorials are private choices. Here we have so few choices' (p. 386).

Throughout the three novels, Berger draws our attention to the material reality of peasant life and of the peasant diaspora of migrant workers across Europe. The prose is characterized throughout by its attentiveness to physical detail. It obliges us to see what the characters in the novels see, but also to take into account their ways of seeing. We are invited to see the world in immediate physical terms and to see it as if we ourselves were in attendance. In *Pig Earth*, for example, the emphasis on the generative cycle focuses on specific instances of slaughter or, as in the following passage, birth:

> Two of the calf's hooves were already visible. Hubert made slip-knots at either end of his rope and passed them over the hooves to the forelegs. Then, with his boots wedged against the gutter, he lay back on the rope and pulled. He saw the calf's head, an eye with long lashes still closed,

> come out. He pulled harder on the rope as until he was almost parallel with the floor. The vagina yawned, and the entire calf emerged like a sound, accompanied by two little rivulets of blood (p. 12)

In this passage – as in so much of Berger's writing – he is asking us to attend to the particularity of things. He is also helping us to understand what it means to be attentive. The brief description is highly visual. We are required to look at Hubert and the cow – to observe them in order to see. We need to look without distraction and, having looked, we need to see. The seeing becomes a kind of understanding and, in this case, requires us to keep a respectful distance. However, we are not dispassionate observers. We understand Hubert's skill in applying the slip knots and the careful effort involved in pulling back on the rope. The birth itself remains beyond our understanding, but we are asked to witness those 'two little rivulets of blood' which acknowledge our human need for empathy. It is as if Hubert, the cow and the as yet unborn calf are being allowed to name themselves – reveal themselves, rather than be revealed through highly wrought prose – and, in naming themselves, allowing us to attend to their predicament.

As the trilogy – in *Lilac and Flag* – follows a younger generation of migrant peasants in search of work and of new lives, Berger employs the same spare prose. The precision of observation is now given to the urban exiles and their efforts to survive in the metropolis. Berger describes the operation of a giant crane with the same attentiveness that, in the earlier volume, he had devoted to the birth of the calf. This final volume, unlike the previous two, is written as a continuous narrative and Berger employs as the fictional narrator an old woman who is still in touch with the traditional peasant culture. The story concerns two young lovers: a girl, Zsuzsa (a stripper with a brother who deals in drugs), and a boy, Sucus (an aspiring crane driver who becomes drawn into crime). The city they live in – a sprawling, unidentified capital with suburbs named after those of big cities across the world – assumes mythic proportions. It is as if Europe had become one great sprawling, interconnected wasteland of urban desolation.

The tension in the novel lies in our having to acknowledge that the love between Sucus and Zsuzsa is sincere and altruistic, but at the same time doomed both by their own actions and by the force of circumstance. The situation it depicts with unsparing honesty is tragic – tragic in the sense that, as we shall see in Chapter 7, Martha Nussbaum employs that term – because it shows the everyday facts of human vulnerability and frailty in the face of the inevitable contingency and the incommensurability of the human condition. At the end of *Lamb and Flag*, Sucus, who has been searching for the missing

Zsuzsa, suddenly stopped in front of a shop window to look at 'a jersey dress, tight-fitting, with black spots like a panther':

> He simply stood there without moving, for a year, and towards the end of that time he learnt that only a body can forgive a body, and that forgiveness, if it comes, comes with a honeycomb of tenderness secreted by the bodies concerned. His eyes shut before the shop window; he saw how forgiveness could never be the consequence of judgment. Forgiveness was not a principle, but a brush of lips on closed eyes. The prefix *for* in *forgievan*, Old English, meant, like the Greek *peri*, enclosing, encircling, embracing (p. 506).

Berger himself does not judge. He does not believe that Sucus is any of the names with which we might label him: 'conman', 'criminal', 'stray', 'victim', etc. He knows that the minutes spent in front of the shop window were, for Sucus, a year – not a life time (life had to go on), but not minutes either (time, for Sucus, had stalled). He knows, also, that we can never know what that 'year' meant for Sucus. But he shows how that insight into the nature of forgiveness is one that we – the reader, the author, the narrator and Sucus – all share. We have that in common at least. We are all from our very different perspectives drawn into a shared understanding – for a minute, or a year, or however long it takes.

Brief as Photos

> *Memory is not unilinear at all. Memory works radically, that is to say with an enormous number of associations all leading to the same event.* (Berger, 1980, 60)

As Said pointed out, photography is central to Berger's intellectual and artistic project. Photographs document social reality while at the same time disrupting it. They fix memory in particular moments of time, but on the understanding that 'memory is not unilinear'. Indeed, argues Berger in his essay on 'Uses of Photography' quoted above, memory disrupts the linearity of time. 'If we want to put a photograph back into the context of experience, social experience, social memory', he continues, 'we have to respect the laws of memory. We have to situate the printed photograph so that it acquires something of the surprising conclusiveness of that which *was* and *is*' (p. 61).

Early on in his career, Berger collaborated with Jean Mohr in developing photographic accounts of everyday life. *A Fortunate Man* (1967) and *A*

Seventh Man (1975) established that collaboration as pivotal in the development of Berger's oeuvre (see Berger and Mohr, 1967; 1975). The former tells the story, in photographs and short narratives, of a country doctor, his work and his encounters with his patients; the latter is a book of Mohr's photographic images and Berger's multi-layered commentary about migrant workers in Europe. In both, the collaboration reinforces the complementarity of word and photographic image, although, in *A Seventh Man*, there is a sense that Berger's analysis is shaping the form and sequence of the book as he works towards the elaboration of similar themes in *Into Their Labours*.

Some of Berger's most compelling works use photography as a metaphor for the instantaneity of the visual arts: their capacity to arrest time in a moment of concentrated visual intensity. *And Our Faces, My Heart, Brief as Photos* (1984) achieves this concentration through a reflection on time and space as expressed through Berger's prose and poetry. *Photocopies* (1996) uses still-life images as a starting point for a kind of memoir: a reflection on self through the images that constitute that self. *The Shape of a Pocket* (2001) uses photographs as a way of reflecting on the possibility of resistance to a new world economic order that effaces faces. Photography not only captures the moment in such a way as to fuse space and time in an instant, but also does so through a medium and a technology which is common and ordinary and part of many people's everyday culture. It is one of the least elite and most recent art forms and as such is an appropriate medium for Berger who positions himself very clearly and explicitly on the democratic socialist left of politics.

Photography has also an international form with a very strong tradition of documenting social conditions and events. It is perhaps increasingly associated with the fashion industry, with celebrity culture and with the full spectrum of photo-journalism. However, it has important roots in social realism. It can be – and has been – used with great effect to reveal the harsh realities that lie concealed beneath the ideological myths. Photography has the capacity to tell it as it is – although, of course, it can be used to present a highly distorted view of how it is. It is always, however, one of our most powerful and accessible 'ways of seeing'. As George Szirtes (2011), the poet and translator, suggests, it has the potential for being one of the most attentive of art forms:

> There is a moment in photography, a decisive moment, to use Cartier Bresson's phrase, when all that happens is that light enters the camera and strikes a sensitive surface. At that moment nothing else can be done.

> At that moment, the world is simply happening. Poets talk of the music of happening: here it is the merest cry. Light enters, registers, makes its mark. The photographer decides nothing: the mechanism of light, material and chemistry take over (pp. 35–36)

The photograph is, in its instantaneity, a rejection of the linearity of time that Berger finds oppressive and that he struggles with in his handling of the narrative form. 'Every conception of history', writes Giorgio Agamben (2007) in his essay on time and history, 'is invariably accompanied by a certain experience of time which is implicit in it, conditions it and thereby has to be elucidated' (p. 99). To challenge history, one must challenge our experience of time, which is precisely what Berger does in his fiction. 'It is certainly no accident', continues Agamben, 'that every time modern thought has come to reconceptualise time, it has inevitably had to begin with a critique of continuous, quantified time' (p. 112). It is precisely that concept of time as 'continuous, quantified' that photography counters with its 'decisive moment'.

Still-life drawing is, in its processes, quite different from photography, but like photography it is concerned with reclaiming the moment from the linear continuity of time. Berger explains how for him the act of 'drawing is discovery': 'it is the actual act of drawing that forces the artist to look at the object in front of him, to dissect it in his mind's eye and put it together again; or if he is drawing from memory, that forces him to dredge his own mind, to discover the content of his own store of past obeservations' (p. 3). There is nothing instantaneous about this process of discovery. 'A drawing is an autobiographical record of one's discovery of an event – seen, remembered or imagined' (p. 3), states Berger; and, as such, it evolves in and through time, sometimes as a result of a long struggle to 'discover' what one is looking at.

The moment of discovery, as Berger describes it, is not one of completion or accomplishment – of having 'finished' – but of 'crisis':

> A few of the things I recognized, I can describe more directly. I noticed how at the foot of the hard, clenched, weight-bearing leg, there was clear space beneath the arch of the instep. I noticed how subtly the under-wall of the stomach elided into the attenuated, joining planes of thigh and hip. I noticed the contrast between the hardness of the elbow and the vulnerable tenderness of the inside of the arm at the same level. Then, quite soon, the drawing reached its point of crisis (Berger, 2007b, 8).

The leg is a 'hard, clenched, weight-bearing leg'; the elision between stomach, thigh and hip is 'attenuated'; even the perceived 'tenderness' of the inside arm is further qualified with the almost (but not quite) redundant 'vulnerable'. It is as if Berger is being *drawn into* whatever it is that he is trying to *draw out* of his subject. 'We who draw', as he puts it, 'do so not only to make something observed visible to others, but also to accompany something invisible to its incalculable destination' (Berger, 2011, 14). The problem that Berger poses and addresses throughout his work – and that is exemplified in his writing on the practice of drawing – is how to mediate between the self that attends and the subject to which the self gives attention. How can the 'I' that observes not get in the way of the 'the thing' that is being attended to? Berger has no easy answers to that question other than that we need to help one another towards ways of addressing it. The problem for Berger is how not to name the thing before having understood it – or, more accurately, how to understand it by allowing it to name itself.

***

Berger has produced a huge and varied body of work. However, this work extends out from a number of central preoccupations, rather than developing on from a fixed point in the past. It provides us with a landscape that is historically layered, rather than a history with geographical localities. There is, of course, a sense of development in Berger's increasing confidence in handling complex and innovatory forms, but from the outset of his career as a novelist Berger seems to have been clear regarding his intellectual and artistic project and the political implications of that project. Regardless of the genre within which he is working, he is always centrally concerned with attending to the particularity of things in such a way as to preserve and celebrate their unique integrity. For Berger, that process of becoming attentive is a way of positioning oneself politically and personally – a way of seeing that does justice to what it is that we are looking at.

Chapter 6

Becoming Worldly: Edward W. Said (1935–2003)

I still do not know where 'Said' came from, and no one seems able to explain it.
(Said, 1999, 7)

Edward W. Said's entry onto the public scene was a book called *Beginnings*. His final posthumously published text was called *On Late Style*. The former spoke to the relation between 'origins' and 'beginnings' and the latter to the complicated ways in which 'late' plays against expectation and fulfilment. Between his unique beginnings and his immaculate late style, Said provided a highly original body of work covering a diverse range of interests and commitments. The person and the work were all of a piece. They betokened an enormous range and depth of feeling and thought. Despite his diverse commitments, Said possessed an integrity which was rootless with regard to heritage and origin, but deeply rooted in the values of secular humanism. In this chapter, I focus less on the works that Said is perhaps best known for – *Orientalism* and *Culture and Imperialism* – and more on his later work including occasional pieces and published interviews. This choice is partly a result of personal preference and partly a result of the need to focus on those works that speak most directly to my argument.

In the World

What must it be like to be completely at home? I don't know. (Said, 2004a, 236)

Edward W. Said entitled the memoir of his early years 'out of place', and language was for him part of that lifelong experience of displacement:

> Everyone lives life in a given language; everyone's experiences therefore are had, absorbed, and recalled in that language. The basic split in my

> life was the one between Arabic, my native language, and English, the language of my education and subsequent expression as a scholar and teacher, and so trying to produce a narrative of the one in the language of the other – to say nothing of the numerous ways in which the languages were mixed up for me and crossed over from one realm to the other – has been a complicated task (Said, 1999, xv–xvi)

Said was born in Jerusalem, in what was then Palestine, in 1935. By the time of his birth, however, his father was running a family business in Egypt which necessitated the family commuting between Palestine and Egypt. He describes this early experience in an interview conducted in 1996 by Eleanor Wachtel:

> My father was *from* Jerusalem, but he was a rather strange, composite creature . . . . We were always on the move. We would spend part of the year in Egypt, part of the year in Palestine and the summer in Lebanon. In addition to the fact that my father had American citizenship, and I was by inheritance therefore American and Palestinian at the same time, I was living in Egypt and wasn't Egyptian. I, too, was this strange composite, and that's my earliest memory (Said, 2004a, 233–234)

Moreover, as Said goes on to explain in this interview, both his parents were 'Protestants in Palestine'. This meant that his parents, and by implication Said himself, were a minority within a minority: 'they were separated from the overwhelming majority of Christians, who were of course a minority in an essentially Muslim society. Most Christians in the Middle East – or at least in the Levant – are Greek Orthodox' (p. 234). His family compensated for this potential alienation, he explains, 'by creating a cocoon around us. We were unusually different and each of us – my four sisters and I – had different kinds of gifts. And so the result was that we lived in a make-believe world that had no relationship (a) to reality and (b) to the history and actuality of the places we were living in' (pp. 234–235).

He then spent some time, after his family had fled to Cairo in 1947, in a highly exclusive private school where other students included the future King Hussein of Jordan and Michel Shalhoub who would in later life become the actor Omar Sharif. The latter, as Said puts it, 'was rather flashy and daunting in the sense that he used to take it out on smaller kids like myself' (p. 235). The school was run almost entirely by what Said describes as 'shell-shocked veterans of World War II' who upheld the street rule that 'English was the language of the school and if you were caught speaking

Arabic or any other language, you were either caned or given lines or detention' (p. 235). After a few years, the multilingual Said was, in his own words, 'kicked out' (p. 235).

He was then shipped off to what, by his own account, seems an equally awful establishment in the US: 'a disastrously unpleasant puritanical boarding school in New England' (pp. 235–236). As a student, he excelled, but his academic achievements were not recognized. Again, he fell foul of the system. In the 1996 interview on which I am drawing, Said at the age of 57 seems still not to have reconciled himself to this lack of recognition:

> My impression of it was that I was frowned on for my character or absence of it, something of that sort. So, although at the end of two years I graduated as a senior with the highest average in the school, I still wasn't named either salutatorian or valedictorian. When I tried to enquire, I was told that I didn't meet the moral requirements. And I've never forgiven them that particular infringement on my achievement (p. 236)

From then on, as he put it, he did 'all the right things': went to college, graduate school, got a PhD, got a job, obtained a fellowship and wrote books. He became a professor at Columbia in 1963, succeeding to Lionel Trilling's chair.

Then, in 1967, the world as he knew it 'completely fell apart':

> More of Palestine, or the rest of Palestine, was taken by the Israelis – the West Bank and Gaza – and I suddenly found myself drawn back to the area.. . . I started to accommodate myself to the repressed or suppressed part of my history which was Arab. I did several things: I started to go back to the Middle East more often; I got married in the Middle East to a Middle Eastern woman; and then in 1972–73 I took a sabbatical year in Beirut, and for the first time in my life undertook a systematic study of Arabic philology and the classics of the Arabic tradition (p. 237)

In 1978, his major work, *Orientalism,* was published and made him world famous. (It is now translated into 36 languages). In the previous year, he had become a member of the Palestinian National Council and retained his membership till 1991. Not being a member of the Palestine Liberation Organization (PLO), he was able to act as go-between in complex and highly sensitive negotiations between the PLO and the Carter administration; negotiations which, with tragic consequences, proved unsuccessful. While deeply critical of the West's indifference to Palestine, he was also outspokenly critical of the leadership of the Palestinian resistance movement. His growing unease with Arafat in particular eventually led to him calling for Arafat to resign, as he made clear in an interview with David Barsamian in1994: 'it's quite obvious that he can't continue' (Said, 2010, 144). In his activism, as in his scholarship, Said clung with great intellectual courage to an insistence on 'belonging and detachment, reception and resistance . . . insider and outsider' (Said, 2004b, 76).

He also understood that this 'task is constitutively an unending one' (p. 77), since there can be no easy, or indeed uneasy, resolution to these ambivalences for the public intellectual who treats that task with seriousness. He was, deeply, and in a manner at odds with the tenor of what Eric Hobsbawm (1995) termed 'the short twentieth century', not only a humanist but a humanist whose scholastic and political actions and reflections turned always to humaneness, tolerance and recognition – or, as he put it, to 'an exfoliating, elaborating, demystifying general humaneness' (Said, 2004b, 81).

In early September 1991, Said convened a seminar in London of Palestinian intellectuals and activists drawn from 'all over the Palestinian world – the West Bank and Gaza, the Palestinian diaspora in various Arab countries, Europe and North America'. The idea of the conference was 'to try to articulate a common set of themes that would enhance the course of our progress toward self-determination as a people'. What transpired from the seminar 'was a terrible disappointment: the endless repetition of well-known arguments, our inability to fix on a collective goal, the apparent desire to listen only to our ourselves'. During the course of that seminar Said learnt from his New York physician that he was suffering from chronic lymphocytic leukaemia. He learnt that he was dying (see Said, 1999, 214).

The last decade of Said's life was in many ways his most active and creative, despite his worsening medical condition. In 1993, he delivered the Reith Lectures, *Representations of the Intellectual* (Said 1994), which provoked strong and mixed responses (see Collini, 2006, 422–432; Veeser, 2010, 194–203). While producing some of his most original academic work, he also established with Daniel Barenboim the West-Eastern Divan Workshop, which brought together talented young musicians between the ages of fourteen to twenty-five from Egypt, Syria, Lebanon, Jordan, Tunisia and Israel and established itself as a permanent orchestra (Barenboim and Said, 2003). He also continued to write regular essays and articles on music for *The Nation* and other publications (Said, 2009) and contribute a column to an Arab language outlet, the Cairo newspaper *Al-Ahram*, on US policy in the

Middle East and what he saw as the failure of the Arab leadership (Said, 2004c). The unity amidst this highly creative complexity of interest and concern was the deeply rooted humanism – his sense of being out of place and in the world – of his own rootless cosmopolitanism.

The World in the Book

> *. . . a sympathetic dialogue of two spirits across ages and cultures who are able to communicate with each other as friendly, respectful intelligences trying to understand each other from the other's perspective* (Said, 2004b, 92)

Background, as Said understood and used the term, is not just a matter of life events as briefly sketched above. It is also a matter of how a life relates to other lives and how those complex relations are historically embedded in the material 'stuff' of cultural reproduction. Background asserts itself into the foreground. For Said, whose life was pre-eminently that of a scholar, writer and public intellectual, that embedding and foregrounding necessarily involve a kind of ongoing conversation with other works and other minds. Said defined himself as a 'democratic humanist' and maintained that his life as such 'is about reading, it is about perspective, and . . . it is about transitions from one realm, one area of human experience to another. That deployment of an alternative identity is what we do when we read and when we go on to expand the area of attention to include widening circles of pertinence' (Said, 2004b, 80). To understand the life of such a person we have ourselves, therefore, to attend to these 'widening circles of pertinence'.

As Said (2004b) makes clear, he was consciously writing within, and sometimes against, what he saw as a clearly delineated scholarly tradition of philological hermeneutics reaching back to Giambattista Vico in the eighteenth century. Vico's great contribution to hermeneutics, through the publication of *New Science* in 1744, was the idea of an 'epoch' as being somehow self-defining and coherent in terms of its complex interconnectivities and interpretive modes. That, according to Said, is why our understanding of words matters and the contexts within which they are used matter; it is why philology as a sociological and historical mode of enquiry matters and continues to matter. What words are doing, what designs they might have upon us, can only be understood from within their own world; which is not only a world of semantic and synchronic structure, but also a world of dialectical and diachronic development. The world is the book. (See Curtius, 1990, 302–347).

One of the greatest twentieth century exponents of this scholarly tradition, according to Said (2004b), was Erich Auerbach, whose *Mimesis: the Representation of Reality in Western Literature* was written in German in Istanbul during World War II and first appeared in English translation in the United States in 1953. Auerbach was a Jew – a German Jew writing with bare scholastic resources at a time of grave personal danger and insecurity – and his book is, in Said's words, 'an exile's book' (Said, 2004b, 97). Said argues that Auerbach conceptualized a 'new figural dispensation' (p. 107) whose 'representation of reality' constituted a radical break from both the pre-Christian past and the ensuing period during which the status of Latin as the lingua franca of Europe was gradually eroded. Central to that dispensation was the notion of both history and language as dynamic, unpredictable and not-yet-finished. Suspense became an indispensable element of the human storyline and required, for its adequate representation, new vernaculars: Italian, in the case of Dante; Norman English in the case of Chaucer; Modern English in the case of Milton.

This 'new figural dispensation' allows history to talk back to itself; to respect linearity, while seeking to resolve deep historical divides through a different conceptualization of time; as when, for example, the Old Testament is seen as foreshadowing the New Testament and the New Testament as echoing the Old Testament: 'the past realized in the present, the present prefiguring as well as acting like a sort of eternal redemption' (Said, 2004b, 109). To read back into the story of Abraham and Isaac a later story of the crucifixion of the 'Son of Man' is to reinterpret it; and to relate that later Christian story to the older Jewish story is to enrich our understanding of both (and, sometimes, as in the case of Kierkegaard's treatment of the older story, in *Fear and Trembling*, to radically recast that understanding). The 'new figural dispensation', according to Said's account of Vico and Auerbach, allows us to read in this way; to connect, that is, across potentially disparate cultural territories.

For Said, the prime focus in any act of reading is on words and what they mean in the context within which they were written or spoken, read or listened to; and on the new contexts within which they have to be reworked. That reworking is essential. It involves, Said reminds us, working our way back into the mind and perspective of the writer and reader. That is precisely why he found writers such as Joseph Conrad and Jane Austen so fascinating and challenging – the critical crux in the latter being Austen's seeming moral disregard for the fact that the slave plantation that Sir Thomas Bertram owns in Antigua is used to finance Mansfield

Park in England. He refuses to dismiss their work as ideologically impure or politically incorrect. 'The foundation of all his work', Paulin (2004, 4) reminds us, 'is the concept of disinterested aesthetic pleasure . . . . He refused to allow his political principles to distort his admiration for particular works of art'.

Instead, insisted Said, works of art that are in dissonance with those 'political principles' need to be read against other post-colonial literatures that speak back to their silences and lacunae:

> There is . . . a whole school of Caribbean writers who, in fact, see the imperial experience in its past – as slave colonies – from a completely different perspective than Jane Austen. What I'm saying is that the fullest and most interesting way to read people like Jane Austen or later Kipling, who writes about India, is to see them not only in terms of English novels but also in terms of these other novels which have come out. You can read them contrapuntally to use the metaphor for music. They are going over the same history but from a different point of view. When you read them that way, you get a sense of the interdependence of these normally quarantined literatures. There's nothing more exciting and interesting than that (Said, 2004a, 244–245)

Said was adamant that interpretation of texts involves locating them within their own historical contexts and understanding them in relation to those contexts – understanding them, that is, on their own historical terms. He sought to understand texts in their historical contexts, but not to view those texts simply as the products of historical determination. Interpretation thereby becomes a matter of balancing authorial agency against historical structure – a matter of understanding the process of 'structuration' as evidenced in specific texts. Said (2004b, 62) makes the general point in the following terms: 'for the humanist, the act of reading is the act therefore of first putting oneself in the position of the author, for whom writing is a series of decisions and choices expressed in words'. That 'first' is an important qualifier, since, as Said goes on to argue, there is a secondary requirement in any serious attempt at interpretation: 'no author is completely sovereign or above the time, place and circumstances of his or her life, so that these, too, must be understood if one is to put oneself in the author's position sympathetically'

Said instantiates this general point with reference to the work of Joseph Conrad, whose novella, *The Heart of Darkness*, written between 1898 and 1899, had been attacked as racist by Chinua Achebe in the second

Chancellor's Lecture delivered at the University of Massachusetts in 1975 (Achebe, 2010). It was, declared Achebe, 'an offensive and deplorable book' (p. 16). For Said (2004a, 62–63), however, 'to read an author like Conrad . . . is first of all to read his work as if with the eye of Conrad himself, which is to try to understand each word, each metaphor, each sentence as something consciously chosen by Conrad in preference to any number of other possibilities'. Such reading, as Said goes on to argue, involves 'getting inside his language so as to speak, inside it so as to understand why he put it that way in particular, to understand it as it was made'. Once having got inside that language – 'each word, each metaphor, each sentence' – one sees that the cognitive intelligence at work is complicatedly embroiled, 'in a state of unreconciled opposition', with the ideological cross currents and material conditions of its time.

Said returns to Conrad over and over again in his writing with increasingly close and nuanced readings of *Heart of Darkness* in particular: 'I have found myself over the years reading and writing about Conrad like a *cantus firmus*, a steady ground bass to much that I have experienced' (Said, 2000, 555). Conrad was the subject of his first book published in 1966: *Joseph Conrad and the Fiction of Autobiography*; and almost thirty years later he prefaced *Culture and Imperialism* with a quotation from *Heart of Darkness* and developed further his complex and subversive reading of this classic text. Focusing on the circularity of the narrative whereby the narrator, Marlow, begins and ends his story of 'darkest Africa' sitting on board a boat at the mouth of the Thames waiting for the tide to turn as the light fades, Said is able to see it from the historical perspective of both Conrad and his contemporary reader. Referring to Marlow, a seaman and wanderer who tells the story, and Kurtz, the power-crazed ivory trader who is the principle subject of the story, Said writes:

> They (and of course Conrad) are ahead of their time in understanding that what they call 'the darkness' has an autonomy of its own, and can reinvade and reclaim what imperialism had taken for *its* own. But Marlow and Kurtz are also creatures of their time and cannot take the next step, which would be to recognize that what they saw, disablingly and disparagingly, as a non-European 'darkness' was in fact a non-European world *resisting* imperialism so as one day to regain sovereignty and independence, and not, as Conrad reductively says, to re-establish the darkness . . . . As a creature of his time, Conrad could not grant the natives their freedom, despite his severe critique of the imperialism that enslaved them (original emphases) (Said, 1993a, 33–34)

For Said, interpretation involves reading and re-reading over decades and with enormous attention to both the form of the text and to its ' individual particular, without which there can be no real literature, no utterance worth making and cherishing, no human history and agency fit to protect and encourage' (Said, 2004b, 80). It was as a result of that kind of interpretive endeavour sustained over time and tested against one's own experience that Said was able to show how Conrad's great novella is ideologically at odds with the imperialist ideology in which it is embedded and which it both reproduces and challenges. To read a novel written in a particular context and the last decade of the nineteenth century as if it had been written in an entirely different context and in the late twentieth century is to misunderstand the nature and purpose of interpretation. 'A great effort has to be made', argues Said (1997a, 164), 'to pierce the barriers that exist between one situation, the situation of the interpreter, and another, the situation that existed when and where the text was produced'. The world that is in the book may be a very different world than the one the reader inhabits. The task of interpretation is to span those two worlds through an understanding of both: an understanding, that is, of one's own situation as interpreter and of the situation of that which is being interpreted. The greater the distance between those two situations the greater the interpretive task.

The Book in the World

> *No interpretation is without precedents or without some connection to other interpretations.* (Said, 1997a, 163)

There are interesting lines of continuity and solidarity between the views advanced by Said and those of Quentin Skinner (2003) whose lifelong work on the history of art and ideas – and their inter-relation – is based upon the assumption that the individual text can only be understood in relation to other texts: 'to argue is always to argue for or against a certain assumption or point of view or course of action. It follows that, if we wish to understand such utterances, we shall have to find some means of identifying the precise nature of the intervention constituted by the act of uttering them' (I, 115). All texts, according to Skinner, are part of an ongoing argument and the task of the reader is to locate the text within that broader deliberative process. Interpretation necessarily involves close and critical reading across diverse texts, rather than an exclusive absorption in the individual text itself. The quality of our reading is, crucially, dependent upon our capacity to connect; to read across normally quarantined literatures; to think beyond the received differences and the assumed continuities; to be constantly alert to the vagaries of background. Our readings – of books, of texts, of artefacts – are always complicatedly located in the world.

To understand the text, we have to understand something of the argumentative debate of which it is a constitutive element: the contested terrain of ideas and interests, always powerfully controlled and constrained, within which the text is located and against which it anxiously seeks to exert its influence. 'World', 'worldly', 'worldliness' and the related 'cosmopolitan' and 'cosmopolitanism' are key words in Said's critical lexicon. They highlight the interconnectivity of texts, the complex web of social relations that bind and distinguish them and the need for global and trans-national perspectives in our reading of social reality and the political options that are open to us. As Said (2004a, 26) puts it in an early interview: 'to reintegrate himself with worldly actuality, the critic of texts ought to be investigating the system of discourse by which the "world" is divided, administered, plundered, by which humanity is thrust into pigeon-holes, by which "we" are "human" and "they" are not, and so forth'. He adds: 'we will discover that even so innocuous a discipline as philology has played a crucial role in the process'.

Important assumptions underlie this approach to textual criticism: not least the assumptions that written texts are mutually dependent and that to understand any particular text requires the reader to seek to understand the textual configuration of which it is a constitutive element. There is also the assumption that texts are deliberate interventions: they are actions (complex actions, but actions nonetheless); they are the products of willed agency; expressions of cognitive intelligence. They have designs upon their readers and a vested interest in how related texts are read and interpreted. They are purposefully located by their authors within the constantly evolving polity of letters. Finally, there is the assumption that the world is inescapably wordy: how we understand the world, how we represent it, how we render it knowable, is part and parcel of what the world is and what it becomes.

Said was a practising scholar, teacher, political activist and communicator of exceptional range and depth. Underlying his work is a set of presuppositions – regarding textual authority, historical location and inter-textual resonance – which has tremendous philosophical import regarding the nature of interpretation and the relation between interpretation and textual criticism. It is because texts have authority, and because that authority is always historically located, that they resonate with each other – and with their readers. They invite their readers into their conversations. The reader is, as it were, ushered into an ongoing argument and invited, first, to understand what is going on ('to find some means of identifying the precise nature of the intervention constituted by the act of uttering them', as Skinner, 2002, 115, puts it); second, to make her or his own purposeful intervention through interpretive criticism; and, third, to go back to the texts and listen again to what is happening between them in the light of previously gained insights and understandings.

To be worthwhile, any interpretation must constitute a new beginning by speaking back to its own interpretive origins. In a lecture, planned as the 2001 Freud Memorial Lecture in Vienna but cancelled on the grounds of 'the political conflict in the Middle East' and subsequently delivered at the Freud Museum of London, Said maintained that 'texts that are inertly of their time stay there: those which brush up unstintingly against historical constraints are the ones we keep with us, generation after generation' (Said, 2003b, 26–27). Interpretations – and every text, regardless of genre, is an interpretation of an interpretation – assert themselves within the interpreted world and in doing so change, if ever so slightly, our interpretation of that world. They take on the world: address it, confront it, challenge it and when necessary oppose it. They refuse its assumption of inevitability. The authority of the text resides not only in the integrity of its internal coherence, but also in its capacity to assert that integrity within and for the world.

For the World

> *Humanism . . . is a technique of trouble, and it must stay that way* (Said, 2004b, 77)

'In order to be able to understand a humanistic text,' argues Said (2004b, 91–92), 'one must try to do so as if one is the author of that text, living the author's reality, undergoing the kind of life experiences intrinsic to the author's life, and so forth, all by that combination of erudition and sympathy that is the hallmark of philological hermeneutics'. But that, of course, is no easy task. It involves what Said termed 'a technique of trouble' which he characterized in terms of two complementary hermeneutic moves: 'reception' and 'resistance'. One has, he maintained, to be sympathetic to the text, while questioning its location within a set of ideological assumptions which are in part embedded within it and in part independent of it. A 'receptive' reading of the text necessarily involves the reader in that kind of 'resistance'. To that extent, as Josipovici (1999, 274) puts it, reading 'is always an act of trust. Suspicion has to follow trust, not precede it. To begin with suspicion is to condemn ourselves to solipsism'.

This is the point at which Said's hermeneutics connects, and is all of a piece with, his politics. However, the distinction between teaching and political action was, for Said, a crucial one. He was particularly insistent that teaching should not be used to proselytize. Of course, teachers may have strong political convictions and may be moved to act on such convictions. Moreover, those convictions may work their way through into the teacher's own understanding of her or his subject. But Said was adamant that, as he put it in an interview with David Barsamian in 1993, teaching should not be seen as a form of politics:

> I don't advocate, and I'm very much against the teaching of literature as a form of politics. I think there's a distinction between pamphlets and novels. I don't think the classroom should become a place to advocate political ideas. I've never taught political ideas in a classroom. I believe that what I'm there to teach is the interpretation and reading of literary texts (Said, 2010, 82)

Nevertheless, for Said, the political action was always informed by understanding. That is what enabled him to speak truth to power with such searing passion, but also with a disinterested authority born of compassion and deep knowledge of the contexts about which he was writing. His anger at the misuse of power is evident in the posthumous collection of occasional essays written between December 2000 and July 2003 and originally addressed to a mainly Arab readership through the Cairo newspaper *Al-Ahram*; but so too is his capacity to listen and learn and, above all, to connect the listening to the learning (see Said, 2004c). His coverage of Middle Eastern politics in the last years of his life show, as Tony Judt (2009, 167) puts it, an urgent commitment to telling 'the world (above all Americans) the truth about Israel's treatment of Palestine; the parallel urgency of getting Palestinians and other Arabs to recognize and accept the reality of Israel and engage with Israelis, especially the Israeli opposition; and the duty to speak openly about the failings of Arab leadership'. The politics, for Said, was in the possibility of mutual understanding across seemingly impossible cultural and political divides.

Such a politics, he consistently maintained, was a matter of 'inclusion and mutual respect' rather than 'exclusivism and belligerence'. Writing in April 2002 at a crucial point in the intensification of American-backed Israeli aggression against Palestine, Said insisted on the importance of knowledge and understanding as essential components of political action:

> There is simply no use operating politically and responsibly in a world dominated by one superpower without having a profound familiarity with the knowledge of that superpower, America, its history, its institutions, its currents and countercurrents, its politics and culture. And above all, a perfect knowledge of its language. . . . We have not at all understood the politics of non-violence. Moreover, neither have we understood the power of trying to address Israelis directly, the way the African National Congress addressed the White South Africans, as part of a politics of inclusion and mutual respect. Coexistence is our answer to Israeli exclusivism and belligerence. This is not conceding: it is creating solidarity and therefore isolating the exclusivists, the racists, the fundamentalists (Said, 2004c, 170–171)

Politics so conceived becomes a deeply deliberative process, the stuff of which is the relentless intransigence of human affairs. The fact that, as he puts it at the opening of the essay quoted above, 'anyone with any connection at all to Palestine is today in a state of stunned outrage and shock' (p. 168) does not absolve those who have such connections of their intellectual responsibility; their responsibility, that is, for channelling that shock and outrage into forms of public expression that open up the debate as to why shocked outrage is a rational response. He is arguing, quite explicitly, for the creation of new solidarities based upon the power of argument, understanding and deliberation: 'America is not monolithic. We have friends, and we have possible friends' (p. 170). The political task is to understand the differences within the seemingly 'monolithic'; to identify the 'friends' and the 'possible friends'; and, by building on those sometimes fragile friendships, to extend the bounds of solidarity.

This humanistic belief in the power of democratic criticism defined Said's diverse interests and commitments. In particular, it shaped his politics in respect of the Middle East and of US policy in relation to the Middle East; and, in so doing, it provided him with the intuition necessary to acknowledge changing circumstances and their inevitable consequences. In the early 1980s, for example, Said was vilified from all sides for advocating a two-state solution to the Israeli-Palestine conflict. Then, in 1988, the Palestinian

National Council belatedly conceded that a two-state solution might be the best one available. But, as Tony Judt (2009, 171) puts it, 'as the years went by, with half of the occupied territories expropriated; with the Palestinian community in shambles and the putative Palestinian territory a blighted landscape of isolated enclaves, flattened olive groves and ruined houses, where humiliated adults were fast losing the initiative to angry, alienated adolescents, Said drew the increasingly irresistible conclusion'.

The 'irresistible conclusion' was that Israel was never going to quit the West Bank and that a singular secular state for Israelis and Palestinians was, therefore, a pragmatic necessity. That conclusion, although signifying a changed position in relation to policy, was entirely congruent with the earlier value position he had advocated and was in accord with his assessment of the situation as it existed. The only way forward was for the Palestinian people, he continued to believe, was to be self-determining and somehow against all the odds to continue in dialogue with their Israeli oppressors. Said's deep commitment to the history and future of the Palestinian people is evident in the portrayal of Palestinian lives that he produced in collaboration with the photographer Jean Mohr under the title of *After the Last Sky* (Said, 1993b). First published in 1986, this book gives a glimpse into whatever it means to live in a kind of double exile: 'wherever we Palestinians are, we are not in our Palestine, which no longer exists' (p. 11). Such exile denies the exiles even the consolation of an anterior reference, since there never was a formally constituted Palestine.

His insistence on the corresponding need, within the Arab community, to go on trying to understand the Israeli exilic history – and its Zionist narrative – is equally apparent in the essays collected in *From Oslo to Iraq and the Roadmap* (Said, 2004c). In a piece collected in that volume and published in May 2001, he clearly stakes out his position: 'I continue to believe as an educator that knowledge – any knowledge – is better than ignorance. There is simply no rational justification from an intellectual point of view for having a policy of ignorance, or using ignorance as a weapon in a struggle. Ignorance is ignorance, no more and no less. Always and in every case' (p. 73). Arguing for shared knowledge and mutual understanding above partisan ignorance and partial understanding – and placing that shared knowledge and mutual understanding in the public domain – was Said's way of doing politics within, and for, the world. In every domain of his public life, Said knew how to distinguish between power and force. He knew that power matters and that force is ultimately self defeating.

In an obituary to his friend and collaborator, Daniel Barenboim (2004) made precisely that point through a musical analogy:

> The difference between power and force is equivalent to the difference between volume and intensity in music. When one says to a musician, 'You are not playing intensely enough', his first reaction is to play louder. And it is exactly the opposite: the lower the volume, the greater the need for intensity, and the greater the volume, the greater the need for a calm force in the sound

There was very little 'volume' in Said. He dressed with great elegance but was never 'loud'; he spoke with passionate intensity, but never shouted; he wrote with precision and – when necessary – with anger, but was never high pitched. In his politics, as in his life, he kept the volume low and the resonance high.

***

In one of his last pieces – published posthumously as *On Late Style* – Said (2006) wrote about the late work of a number of composers, performers and writers that he had returned to throughout his life. The purpose of this collection of essays was to remind his readers that the late work of these artists, far from expressing reconciliation and serenity, was troubled, complex and unprecedented: 'what of artistic lateness not as harmony and resolution, but as intransigence, difficulty and contradiction?' (p. 7). It is difficult not to read Said's own work – particularly his late work – in the light of this commentary. His own 'late style' is at times elegiac, sometimes wryly humorous, always elegantly cosmopolitan and worldly, often white hot with anger at the misuse and abuse of power, but never without hope for the future.

In his 1993 BBC Reith Lectures, Said reminded his listeners that 'speaking the truth to power is no Panglossian idealism: it is carefully weighing the alternatives, picking the right one, and then intelligently representing it where it can do the most good and cause the right change' (Said, 1994, 75). Said was of the world. Homi Bhaba (2005, 7) wrote of his response to news of the death of his friend in terms that evoked both Said's private and public presence, as if the two were inextricably entwined: 'his writings were indestructible, his presence memorable, but the fire and fragility of his voice – the ground note of the "individual particular" from which all human narration begins – would be impossible to preserve for another conversation on literature, music, illness and common friends'.

Chapter 7

Becoming Responsive: Martha C. Nussbaum (b.1947)

There is an intimate connection between the conception of what liberal education involves and the conclusion that it must be extended to all citizens alike.

(Nussbaum, 1997, 31)

Martha C. Nussbaum's work is extensive and varied. Her entry onto the public scene was through the publication of a study of ancient Greek views about how our lives are vulnerable to factors outside our control and how this affects our moral appraisals of one another. The title of that book which was first published in 1986 (a revised and updated edition appeared in 2001) was *The Fragility of Goodness* and its subtitle was 'luck and ethics in Greek tragedy and philosophy'. The substantial body of work that Nussbaum has subsequently produced has developed from this central insight regarding the relation between goodness and frailty. Given that we are vulnerable by nature, then we have a moral responsibility to be responsive to one another's needs. How we become responsive is for Nussbaum a question of great moral significance. Her response to that question has been developed through her continuing work on what is usually referred to as 'the capability approach' which she first developed in close collaboration with Amartya Sen and has applied – with great originality – to the concrete reality of women in India working in conditions of extreme poverty.

Goodness and Vulnerability

> *. . . that much that I did not make goes towards making me whatever I shall be praised or blamed for being; that I must constantly choose among competing and apparently incommensurable goods . . .; that an event that simply happens to me may, without my consent, alter my life . . . – all these I take to be not just the material of tragedy, but everyday facts of lived practical reason.* (Nussbaum, 2001a, 5)

The Fragility of Goodness is a deeply Aristotelian work that draws on Greek tragedy and Greek ethical thought to develop an argument about the nature of human goodness (see Nussbaum, 2001a). Aristotle, argues Nussbaum (drawing for this part of her argument primarily on the *Nicomachean Ethics*), posits two opposing positions in relation to the power of luck and fortune: the luck-supremacy view and agency-supremacy view. One of these positions (luck-supremacy) is that 'living well is just the same thing as having a fortunate life. Good living is a gift of the gods that has no reliable connection with effort, learning, or goodness of stable character' (p. 319). The opposing position (agency-supremacy) is 'that luck has no power at all to influence the goodness of human life. The causal factors relevant to living well . . . are all . . . within the agent's firm grasp; external uncontrolled happenings can neither significantly enhance nor significantly diminish good living.'

Aristotle goes on to dismiss both these extreme positions. However, before outlining Aristotle's position, Nussbaum draws her reader's attention to how Aristotle develops his argument; how, for example, he defines his own position through a careful examination of other opposing positions:

> Aristotle wants to set out these extreme views so that we can ask ourselves what would motivate someone to adopt one of them. This should help us to arrive at a position that does justice to the motivating concerns in each case, while avoiding their excesses and denials. This procedure might be read as a kind of simple-minded conservatism, a mechanical steering of a safe middle course between two dangerous extremes. Carefully examined it is neither simply a middle course nor mechanically pursued. The strategy is to take each extreme view seriously . . . as motivated by something that is really there to be preserved and taken account of. (p. 320)

Throughout, Nussbaum is at pains to offer an explanation not only of what Aristotle understood to be the relation between luck and goodness but also of how he arrived at that understanding and how he seeks to explain that understanding to others. Thus, for example, she points out that the first extreme view on luck (the luck-supremacy view) receives less extensive consideration – 'but the manner in which Aristotle dismisses it is of considerable interest' (p. 320). What, according to Nussbaum, is of 'considerable interest' regarding his rejection of the luck-supremacy view is that it is 'the outcome not of a neutral empirical survey, but of a deliberation in which what we desire to find, what we feel we can live with, enters heavily into practical wisdom's weighing of the alternatives' (p. 320). The luck-supremacy view, in other words, is rejected by Aristotle in its extreme form 'not because it has been found to be at odds with scientific fact about the way things are in the universe, discovered by some value-neutral procedure, but because it strikes a false note'; it is 'too much at odds with our other beliefs, and specifically with our evaluative beliefs about what sort of life would be worth living' (p. 320). Aristotle does not bracket his beliefs in the interest of some 'value-neutral procedure'. He uses those beliefs – those prejudices – as a critical sounding board.

So, Aristotle (according to Nussbaum's exposition) 'wants to investigate and in some way to preserve as true the idea that luck has a serious influence in good life, that the good life is vulnerable and can be disrupted by catastrophe'; but he also wants to preserve the idea 'that the good life should be available by effort' (p. 322). There is, then, 'a gap between being good and living well': the gap between goodness as the consequence of 'actual activity' and the acknowledgement 'that good human activity can be disrupted or decisively impeded by various forms of luck'. His strategy in exploring that gap is, as Nussbaum explains, 'two-pronged': 'against the opponents of luck he will insist on luck's real importance, exploring our belief that it is possible to be dislodged from living well. At the same time, he shows us that, given a conception of good living that values excellences of character and activity according to these, such drastic upsets will be rare.'

The story of Priam (the King of Troy during the Trojan war) is a test case of Aristotle's theory: 'for it begins with a person who had, presumably, developed and maintained a stably virtuous character through life, had acted well and according to excellence – but who was then deprived by war of family, children, friends, power, resources, freedom'. Priam's capacity to act well is diminished because 'he cannot, given the constraints upon him, exercise many of the human excellences for which he was previously known' (p. 328). Priam has, however, 'displayed good character in action consistently through the course of a long life' (p. 329). So, 'Aristotle's challenge', as conceived by Nussbaum, 'is to sketch a response that will do justice to these competing intuitions'.

We are, then, neither the mere victims of luck nor entirely inured to the vagaries and vicissitudes of fortune; we inhabit neither a fatalistic moral universe nor a universe that is shaped exclusively by our own moral ends and purposes. We exist in a tragic universe, within which our individual destinies contend with contingency and plurality:

> The good condition of a virtuous person is not, by itself, sufficient for full goodness of living. Our deepest beliefs about value, when scrutinized, show us that we require more. We require that the good condition find its

> completion or full expression in activity; and this activity takes the agent to the world, in such a way that he or she becomes vulnerable to reversals . . . The vulnerability of the good person is not unlimited . . . But the vulnerability is real. (p. 340)

Our response to the tragic human condition – the condition, that is, of moral agency worked out through contingency and incommensurability within the everyday facts of lived practical reason – involves what Nussbaum calls 'relational goods': the goods of membership and association, of friendship and filial association and of intimacy and love (pp. 343–371). If frailty is part of the human condition – part of the 'everyday facts of lived practical reason' – then mutual responsiveness to our shared frailty becomes a necessary condition for human sustainability. Nussbaum develops this notion of responsiveness to the shared human condition in the work that followed from *The Fragility of Goodness*. To be fully human is to be responsive.

Responsiveness and Relationality

> *Emotions are forms of* intentional awareness*: that is . . ., they are forms of awareness* directed at *or* about *an object, in which the object figures as it is seen from the creature's point of view.* (original emphases) (Nussbaum, 1994, 80)

The relation between fragility, goodness and responsiveness is one of the recurring themes throughout Nussbaum's work. It threads its way through, for example, her hugely influential *Love's Knowledge: Essays on Philosophy and Literature* (1990) and her *The Therapy of Desire: Theory and Practice in Hellenistic Ethics* (1994). However, for the purposes of this argument, I shall concentrate on her *Upheavals of Thought: The Intelligence of Emotions* (2001), which traces human intelligence back to its origins in what she sees as the unique frailty and vulnerability of human infancy (see Nussbaum, 2001b). The emotions, for Nussbaum, play a crucial role in the development of human intelligence and in our capacity as sentient beings for responsiveness to others.

This remarkable book – which is almost impossible to define with regard to its academic genre – opens with a personal story about what she calls 'need and recognition'. The story is highly germane to the ensuing argument. In 1992, Nussbaum was, she tells us, lecturing at Trinity College, Dublin. Her mother was in hospital convalescing after 'a serious but routine operation' and so Nussbaum phoned at regular intervals to receive reports on her mother's progress. During one of those phone calls, she received information that her mother was unexpectedly in a life-threatening condition – 'her life was in jeopardy'. 'This news', Nussbaum tells us, 'felt like a nail suddenly driven into my stomach'. She took the next return flight available, but this was not until the following day. So she delivered her scheduled lecture that evening and in the night had a dream in which her mother 'said that others might call her wonderful, but she very much preferred to be called beautiful':

> During the transatlantic flight the next day, I saw, with hope, that image of health before me. But I also saw, more frequently, the image of her death, and my body wanted to interpose itself before that image, to negate it. With shaking hands I typed out paragraphs of a lecture on mercy, and the narrative understanding of criminal offenders. And I felt, all the while, a vague and powerful anger – at the doctors, for allowing this crisis to occur, at the flight attendants, for smiling as if everything were normal, above all at myself, for not having been able to stop this event from happening, or for not having been there with her when it did. (p. 20)

Arriving in Philadelphia, Nussbaum was informed that her mother had died 20 minutes earlier. Nussbaum then describes her reaction in the weeks that followed: 'agonized weeping; whole days of crushing fatigue; nightmares in which I felt altogether unprotected and alone; and seemed to feel a strange animal walking across my bed' (pp. 20–21). She acknowledges the 'urgency and heat' of these emotions, 'their tendency to take over the personality' and their 'apparently adversarial relation to "rationality" in the sense of cool calculation or cost-benefit analysis'. In the light of these features, as Nussbaum herself acknowledges:

> It might seem strange to suggest that emotions are forms of judgement. And yet it is something close to this thesis that I shall defend. I shall argue that all these features not only are compatible with, but actually are explained by, a modified version of the Greek Stoic view, according to which emotions are forms of evaluative judgement that ascribe to certain things and persons outside a person's own control great importance for the person's own flourishing. Emotions are thus, in effect, acknowledgements of neediness and lack of self-sufficiency. (p. 22)

The central point of Nussbaum's argument is that we share as human beings a unique experience of prolonged helplessness in infancy and, during that same period, a unique experience of cognitive growth. We rely unconditionally on others, during the formative period of our human intelligence, to supply our every need. We are entirely the centre of our own infant universe which is entirely beyond our control. Our emotions originate in this tension between helplessness and omnipotence and the 'upheaval' occasioned by that tension. This 'upheaval', argues Nussbaum, focuses the infant on particular objects of desire, shame, or disgust: on what is salient within its own field of perception. It selects from that field of perception that which will meet its basic needs. In the 'upheaval' occasioned by the conjuncture of unconditional helplessness and unconditional demand lie the bases of human judgement.

There is, then, a 'cognitive content' of emotions that resides in their history – a 'cognitive content' that (following Bowlby, 1973; 1980; 1982; and Winnicott, 1965; 1986) she insists would not be possible without a history of responsiveness born of human incompletion and frailty:

> Adult human emotions cannot be understood without understanding their history in infancy and childhood. For this history will bring to light the responsiveness of the emotions – their appropriateness to the life of an incomplete creature in a world of significant accidents, their connections to the development of practical reason and a sense of self – and their frequent lack of responsiveness, their rigidity before present objects as they project the images of the past upon them. (p. 178)

Faced with the sheer unpredictability and contingency of the human world into which we are born – and our own powerlessness in relation to that experience of unpredictability and contingency – we learn to be responsive to one another's needs and wants: to develop 'forms of awareness *directed at* or *about* an object'. This '*intentional awareness*', as Nussbaum terms it in the quotation that heads this section, is rooted in our emotions. The emotions play a crucial role in the development of our selves and others as sentient and responsive beings. However, for that development to be sustainable, argues Nussbaum, human beings require what she calls 'capabilities'. Without these capabilities, development stalls and human flourishing is impossible. The capabilities that Nussbaum specifies, elaborates and instantiates constitute the conditions necessary for that flourishing. We become responsive by becoming capable – and we express our responsiveness to others by enabling them to acquire the capabilities necessary for them to fulfil their human potential.

The 'Central Capabilities'

> *The person with plenty of food may always choose to fast, but there is a great difference between fasting and starving, and it is this difference that I wish to capture.* (Nussbaum, 2000, 87)

Nussbaum's more recent work has focused on capabilities and 'the capabilities approach' to human development – or, more succinctly, 'the human development approach'. Her work in this area is closely aligned to that of Amartya Sen and much of that work is collaborative (see, for example, Nussbaum and Sen, 1993). However, Nussbaum has been at pains to distinguish her approach from that of Sen, while acknowledging his contribution to her own thinking in this area. Some of these distinctions – and, indeed, the terminology associated with them – have remained somewhat fuzzy, but in her *Creating Capabilities: The Human Development Approach* (2011), she spells out her position with great clarity. She distinguishes her approach from what she calls 'the GDP approach' (whereby the progress of a country is viewed solely by economic growth as measured by GDP per capita), aligns it with what she terms 'human rights approaches' (whereby development is viewed with reference to a wider range of economic, social and political entitlements) and distinguishes it from that of Sen through what she sees as the need to specify certain 'central capabilities' (whereby certain 'fundamental entitlements' are judged to be universal, although subject to local, regional and national modification and negotiation).

In defining 'capabilities', she makes a further set of distinctions between 'basic capabilities', 'combined capabilities' and 'internal capabilities' and between 'capabilities' and 'functionings'. That last distinction – between 'capabilities' and 'functionings' – is crucial. Particular functionings cannot simply be read off against their associated capabilities, because capability involves choice: the choice as to how, and whether, we are to actualize that capability. Without freedom of choice, Nussbaum insists, capability is reduced to mere functioning; freely chosen, functioning is an expression of our capability. Capabilities 'are the answers to the question, "What is this person able to do and be?" In other words, they are not only just abilities residing inside a person but also the freedoms or opportunities created by a combination of personal abilities and the political, social and economic environment' (p. 20). Capabilities function in combination – hence, the idea of 'combined capabilities'.

The distinction between 'combined capabilities' and 'internal capabilities' is not sharp, but is nevertheless significant in Nussbaum's schema: 'combined capabilities are defined as the internal capabilities plus the social/political/economic conditions in which functioning can actually be chosen' (p. 22). The distinction draws our attention to the importance of, for example, educating people so that they are capable of free speech and providing them free expression in practice. Unless we are able to actualize our 'internal capabilities' in functioning combinations, we lack the freedom to develop and flourish to our full potential. These 'internal capabilities' are not innate, which is why Nussbaum introduces the category of 'basic capabilities': 'basic capabilities are the innate faculties of the person that make later development and training possible' (p. 24). Within this schema, we infer 'basic capabilities' from a process – that begins with birth (and arguably before birth) – whereby 'internal capabilities' find their fulfilment and realization in the functioning of 'combined capabilities'. It is that fulfilment and realization that, as Nussbaum puts it, 'deliver to people a life that is worthy of the human dignity that they possess' (p. 30).

The point of this somewhat complex set of distinctions is to insist on the actualization of capability through the exercise of free choice. On this central point, Nussbaum is in agreement with Sen (1999). Where she differs from Sen is in her insistence on the need to employ a threshold or specific list of capabilities. Sen does see some capabilities – such as health, education, political participation, non-discrimination – as more important than others, but does not identify a specific set of capabilities as having universal relevance or applicability. The reason that Nussbaum does specify a list of what she calls 'Central Capabilities' is because of the necessary relation she sees between freedom and justice: 'some freedoms involve basic social entitlements, and others do not. Some lie at the heart of a view of political justice, and others do not. Among the ones that do not lie at the core, some are simply less important, but others may be positively bad' (p. 72). The promotion of freedom as an end in itself is incoherent as a political project – we need to understand which freedoms we are seeking to promote.

From Nussbaum's point of view, then, it is essential to specify those capabilities most likely to provide the freedoms upon which a just society might be based. It is in the context of this argument that Nussbaum presents the 'ten Central Capabilities'. These inform her *Women and Human Development: The Capabilities Approach* (2000) and her *Frontiers of Justice: Disability, Nationality, Species Membership* (2006), and are discussed in more general terms in *Creating Capabilities*:

1. *Life.* Being able to live to the end of a human life of normal length . . .
2. *Bodily health.* Being able to have good health, including reproductive health . . .

3. *Bodily integrity.* Being able to move freely from place to place; to be secure against violent assault . . .
4. *Senses, imagination and thought.* Being able to use the senses, to imagine, think and reason . . .
5. *Emotions.* Being able to have attachments to things and people outside ourselves . . .
6. *Practical reason.* Being able to form a conception of the good and to engage in critical reflection about the planning of one's life . . .
7. *Affiliation.* (A) Being able to life with and towards others . . . (B) Having the social bases of self-respect and non-humiliation . . .
8. *Other species.* Being able to live with concern for and in relation to animals, plants and the world of nature.
9. *Play.* Being able to laugh, to play, to enjoy recreational activities.
10. *Control over one's environment.* (A) *Political.* Being able to participate effectively in political choices that govern one's life . . . (B) Material. Being able to hold property . . ., and having property rights on an equal basis with others . . .

(Nussbaum, 2011, 33–34; Nussbaum, 2000, 78–80)

Among these 'capabilities', which Nussbaum sees as essential to human well being, she privileges what she terms 'affiliation' and 'practical reasoning': 'they both organize and suffuse all the others, making their pursuit truly human'. Citing work as an example, she argues that 'work, to be a truly human mode of functioning, must involve the availability of both practical reason and affiliation. It must involve being able to behave as a thinking being, not just a cog in a machine; and it must be capable of being done with and towards others in a way that involves mutual recognition of humanity' (Nussbaum, 2000, 82). Work requires of the worker both a conception of the good and the capacity to apply that conception, through practical reasoning, to particular ends and purposes. So, for example, if I am a medical practitioner, I seek through practical reason to align my practice to the ends and purposes of healing; if I am a lawyer, I seek to align it to those of justice; if I am a teacher, to those of learning. Professional practice, insists Nussbaum, requires a sense of moral purposefulness on behalf of the practitioner. Practical reason is the means whereby the practitioner meets this moral requirement; the means, that is, whereby practice becomes morally purposeful and purposes are imbued with practical import.

In defining 'affiliation', Nussbaum draws a distinction between, on the one hand, being 'able to imagine the situation of another and to have compassion for that situation; to have the capability for justice and friendship', and, on the other hand, of 'being able to be treated as a dignified being whose worth is equal to that of others; . . . being able to work as a human being, exercising practical reason and entering into meaningful relationships of mutual recognition with other workers' (Nussbaum, 2011, 34; Nussbaum, 2000, 79–80). What emerges from this distinction is the importance of reciprocity: the way in which 'the capability for justice and friendship' is crucially dependent upon 'being able to be treated as a dignified human being whose worth is equal to that of others'. My capability for justice and friendship towards others is, in other words, dependent upon the capability of others for justice and friendship towards me. The capability of 'affiliation', like that of 'practical reason', is fundamental because without it there is no way of ensuring that our other capabilities can become functional.

The Capabilities and Education

> *Play is not play if it is enforced, love is not love if it is commanded.* (Nussbaum, 2000, 88)

In emphasizing the importance of education within 'the capabilities approach', Nussbaum draws attention to its pivotal role in drawing a range of capabilities into combined and mutually supportive functionings. Drawing on a concept introduced by Wolff and De-Shalit (2007), she categorizes education as a 'fertile functioning' (i.e. one that tends to promote other related functionings):

> Education . . . forms people's existing capacities into developed *internal capabilities* of many kinds. This formation is valuable in itself and a source of lifelong satisfaction . . . It is also pivotal to the development and exercise of many other human capabilities: a 'fertile functioning' of the highest importance in addressing disadvantage and inequality. People who have received even a basic education have greatly enhanced employment options, chances for political participation, and abilities to interact productively with others in society, on a local, national, and even global level. (Nussbaum, 2011, 152)

In order for education to facilitate this 'fertile function', there may, she argues, be a need to relax the emphasis placed on choice elsewhere within her version of the 'the capabilities approach'. In the education of children in particular, but also of young people in higher education, there is a need to require functioning – not simply capability. She is not here arguing for didactic modes of teaching: her *Cultivating Humanity: A Classical Defence of Reform in Liberal Education* (1997) and her *Not for Profit: Why Democracy Needs the Humanities* (2010) provide staunch defences of what she calls 'Socratic pedagogy' which highlights the importance of 'the narrative imagination' and actively promotes 'the study of non-Western cultures', 'women's studies' and 'the study of human sexuality'. She also draws on the educational thought and practice of John Dewy and Rabindranath Tagore in developing her ideas on global citizenship and its implications for education. Her point is that an element of compulsion is justified in the education of young people given that it 'is such a pivotal factor in opening up a wide range of adult capabilities' (Nussbaum, 2011, 156) – and in opening up those capabilities 'to all citizens alike' as she puts it in the key statement that heads this chapter.

One implication of this re-emphasis is the need for a broad and balanced curriculum for all. Again, she is not denying the importance of an element of choice, but is arguing for a curriculum with the capacity for 'cultivating humanity': 'our campuses educate our citizens. Becoming an educated citizen means learning a lot of facts and mastering techniques of reasoning. But it means something more. It means learning how to be a human being capable of love and imagination.' The re-emphasis, in other words, is less on the narrowing of choice and more on the broadening and deepening of educational provision, so that we do not 'continue to produce narrow citizens who have difficulty in understanding people different from themselves, whose imaginations rarely venture beyond their local setting' (Nussbaum, 1997, 14). A point conveniently overlooked by those peddling the slogan of 'free choice' is that 'choice' cannot be 'free' when it is constrained by economic factors that limit the choices available and/or by lack of information regarding the implications of the choices on offer.

So, while Nussbaum does not specify a particular curriculum framework, she clearly places a strong emphasis on breadth and balance. Those arguing this case are frequently dismissed as defenders of a liberal arts tradition that reached its apotheosis in the US liberal arts colleges. However, Nussbaum is not defending a particular kind of historically located US institution. She is arguing that all young people engaged in higher education are entitled to a curriculum that introduces them to the wonders of science and the precision of art. For example, her (1995) *Poetic Justice: The Literary*

Imagination and Public Life, which shows how novels and novel reading can shape our conception of public reasoning, developed from her legal teaching in the law school at the University of Chicago:

> The subject of my legal teaching was, in fact, storytelling, for the course I was asked to teach was Law and Literature. The law students and I read Sophocles, and Plato, and Seneca, and Dickens. In connection with the literary works, we discussed compassion and mercy, the role of the emotions in public judgement, what is involved in imagining the situation of someone different from oneself. We talked about ways in which texts of different types present human beings . . . Since the University of Chicago Law School is the birthplace of the law-and-economics movement, we discussed the relationship between the literary imagination and economic reasoning. (Nussbaum, 1995, xiv)

Nussbaum also places a strong emphasis on motivation and engagement. Volition is supremely important in acquiring the capabilities. Pedagogy, therefore, cannot be based on the assumption that student motivation and engagement already exist – an assumption that is frequently made within and about higher education. Universities must provide not only the appropriate educational opportunities, but also the conditions necessary for student motivation and engagement across a broad diversity of cultural contexts. The achievement of specialist knowledge relating to particular fields of study and the skills necessary to acquire and implement that knowledge – through, for example, scoping, argumentation, analysis, communication – are of supreme importance. However, it is the motivation and engagement of the learner that renders these 'functionings' educationally significant and that transforms the learner into a capable human being: capable, that is, of choosing how to combine and employ these 'functionings' and to what end.

The development of student responsiveness through the development of motivation and engagement are, then, integral to the pedagogic process. Since responsiveness is reciprocal, the teacher's sensitivity to the student is indispensible: 'good education', as Nussbaum (2011, 157) puts it, 'requires sensitivity to context, history, and cultural and economic circumstances'. Every student is different and as far as possible their teachers have a duty to be sensitive to their particular circumstances insofar as these have a bearing on their educational well being. We must all – teachers and students alike – learn 'to see another human being not as a thing but as a full person' (p. 96). It has become part of the professional armoury of some of those working in higher education to dismiss this kind of sentiment as characterizing 'the dangerous rise of therapeutic education' (Ecclestone and Hayes, 2009). However, from Nussbaum's perspective, the danger to education comes not from any supposed super-flux of care, but from a narrowing of perspective whereby the student becomes a mere recipient. That narrowing of the professional horizons enables teachers to view their own practice in more instrumental and therefore manageable terms, but it severely restricts its educational value. What Nussbaum defines as a pedagogical requirement – 'sensitivity to context, history, and cultural and economic circumstances' – makes huge demands on teachers and universities, but is from her perspective a necessary condition of 'good education'.

Responsiveness also involves an acknowledgement of our global interdependency and of the implications of that interdependency. Here, too, Nussbaum sees a clear role for education in the development of what she terms 'citizens of the world' (see Nussbaum, 1997, 50–84; 2011, 79–94). In *Not for Profit*, for example, she highlights the scope of the problems that need to be addressed and for which future generations need to be prepared:

> The problems we need to solve – economic, environmental, religious, and political – are global in their scope. They have no hope of being solved unless people once distant come together and cooperate in ways they have not before. Think of global warming; decent trade regulations; the protection of the environment and animal species; the future of nuclear energy and the dangers of nuclear weapons; the movement of labor and the establishment of decent labor standards; the protection of children from trafficking, sexual abuse, and forced labor. All these can only truly be addressed by multinational discussions. (Nussbaum, 2011, 79–80)

Such a list could, as Nussbaum points out, be extended almost indefinitely. The point is that our problems are increasingly not only collective problems, but also globally collective problems requiring globally collective solutions: problems which at every level of impact – the individual, inter-personal, institutional, national and international – are experienced globally. The collective solutions will emerge not from any totalizing consensus, but from the willingness to reason together and in doing so to acknowledge and respect our differences. 'People love homogeneity and are startled by difference', she writes in her defence of religious equality;

but it is the willingness to be 'startled by difference' that finally wins through in the long haul towards collective solutions. In that same defence – her (2008) *Liberty of Conscience: In Defence of America's Tradition of Religious Equality* – she writes of this long haul as 'the path towards overlapping consensus' (p. 362): the collective, open-ended argument that constitutes deliberative democracy and locates within it mutual respect for our shared human dignity.

Human beings are born with capacities, with potential. What they acquire are the functional capabilities necessary to fulfil that potential. A good society is one which provides the resources necessary for individuals to become functionally capable – to flourish. That functional capability both provides and is premised upon our freedom to choose. We are not born into a state of complete freedom. Our freedom is realized though the capabilities we acquire and the conditions necessary for their acquisition. Luck clearly has a part to play in this, but in a good society policy also plays its part in the fair distribution of capability as it relates to freedom. Notwithstanding her belief that the education of young people is something of a special case with regard to the issue of freedom of choice, Nussbaum is insistent that citizens must be left to determine what they make of the capabilities that are granted them. Capabilities are 'opportunities for functioning' (p. 88), but do not predetermine that functioning. Indeed, the predetermination of function runs the risk of denying the capability of which it purports to be an expression: 'play is not play if it is enforced, love is not love if it is commanded'. Playing, loving – and, indeed, learning – rely unconditionally upon the freedom of those who choose to play, love and learn.

***

The previous four chapters have explored how four very different public educators have worked within what I have termed the interpretive tradition. Each of these public educators has brought something distinctive to that ongoing tradition, while drawing on its intellectual and imaginative resources. This has resulted in a body of work that not only highlights the importance of thoughtfulness, attentiveness, worldliness and responsiveness, but also provides an exemplary record of what it means to become thoughtful, attentive, worldly and responsive. The lives and works documented in those four chapters have integrity in that they exemplify the precepts that they advocate. How could we possibly learn from a thoughtless Hannah Arendt, an inattentive John Berger, a parochial Edward Said or an unresponsive Martha Nussbaum? We ask of them that they should not only espouse their values but also embody them in their practice as public educators. What they ask of us is that we formulate the questions that will enable us to become thoughtful, attentive, worldly and responsive. They ask us to keep the future open through the formulation and pursuit of what is questionable. This is their legacy.

Part Three

Futures

Chapters 8–10 explore some of the institutional implications of that legacy. How might we conceive of a 'pedagogicized university' – a university that, as suggested in the opening chapter, takes pedagogy seriously – if pedagogy is seen as open-ended and indeterminate in its relation to the future, outward-looking and inter-connective in its orientation to the public and deeply respectful of difference in the construction of its own social space? How might such a university organize its curriculum? How might it develop a professional and institutional ethos? How might it view relationality within its own institutional space? These may not be the questions that preoccupy vice chancellors and principals on a daily basis, but they are the questions that need to be addressed if pedagogy is to have a central place within the university and if the university is to play a central role in the development of an inclusive and educated public.

Pedagogy is centrally concerned with the indeterminacy of the relation between past, present and future and the unpredictability of human flourishing that necessarily follows from that indeterminacy. A major consequence of the plurality of the human condition is the impossibility of fully comprehending the outcomes of our own and others' actions – the extent to which and the ways in which our myriad actions interconnect and interrelate. This awareness can lead to a sense of powerlessness, helplessness and a loss of agency or to an inflated sense of one's own power and the need to control events. These polarities of having no control and needing to have total control might be seen as the complementary neuroses of late modernity. The only way to confront and counter those neuroses is through modes of understanding that develop the mutuality and reciprocity of human agency. That development, however, is dependent on institutions that are committed to sustaining those modes of understanding and ensuring the continuity of their traditions.

There is nothing predetermined regarding that continuity other than our determination to ensure it. Our futures are, in part, what we make of them. Whether we can gather them into a common future – of collective aspiration based on shared understanding – remains to be seen. The abject failure of successive governments to acknowledge – let alone confront – the problem of escalating inequality within and across our societies – does not inspire confidence. What does inspire confidence is the possibility of change and renewed momentum within regions and among groups that are facing some of the most severe challenges posed by globalization. Each of the following chapters opens with a vignette that while raising huge questions, nevertheless, points to new beginnings. The future is cosmopolitan and cosmopolitanism requires us both to acknowledge our differences and to recognize our shared humanity. Higher education has a hugely important part to play in securing that future.

Chapter 8

Open Futures

At Birzeit, there would be no weapons. Disagreements had to be resolved by dialogue.
(Gabi Baramki, 2010, 41)

A number of general insights emerge from the previous four chapters. We see, for example, that human understanding is indeterminate in its outcomes. It is a kind of quest. We see also that understanding involves individuation. We become ourselves by understanding the world around us. Finally, we see that understanding is interrogative in form. It takes the form of a question. Each of these insights – although seemingly innocuous – is to varying degrees at odds with the prevailing orthodoxy. Higher education is currently constrained by systems of assessment and accountability that place an undue emphasis on learning outcomes that are specified as predetermined targets, organizational and curriculum structures that offer minimal flexibility and limited entry and exit points, and approaches to teaching and assessment that routinely place students in the role of respondents and recipients of transmitted understanding. This chapter challenges some of the dominant pedagogic assumptions from the perspective of the interpretive tradition as exemplified in the previous four chapters.

Prologue: A University Under Occupation

Birzeit University (BU) is an institution with a history of survival and institutional regeneration. Its only option has been to remain open to the future – or to surrender to what has seemed at times like the inevitability of permanent closure. Founded in 1975, it is located north of Ramallah in the Israeli-occupied Palestinian West Bank. It developed from Birzeit College, which had been created in 1942 as a development of Birzeit Higher School founded in 1924. In 1976, this new University joined the Association of

Arab Universities and the year after it joined the International Association of Universities. It added a Faculty of Commerce and Economics and a Faculty of Engineering before being closed by the military order of the occupying Israeli forces in 1988. It re-opened in 1992 and since then new faculties and centres have been established, including law and public administration, women's studies, media and graduate studies.

Following the enforced deportation of Hanna Nasir, the then president of Birzeit College, in 1974, the vice president Gabi Baramki assumed responsibility for the transition from college to university status. (Hanna Nasir returned and resumed his duties as the president of BU in 1993). Baramki (2010) describes the situation in that transitional and formative period as follows:

> Religious affiliation was not allowed to play a role in the administrations process . . . We did not even ask applicants what their religion was, a policy quite unheard of in our region . . . The student mix we were faced with on the first day of our new degree course reflected our ideals. Streaming into our lecture halls were young people from all backgrounds and from all over: there were modern girls in short skirts from the cities and village girls in long dresses, boys from middle-class homes in new, good-quality shirts and trousers, and boys from refugee camps in faded but carefully ironed clothes. Some had smart watches. Other had never owned one. (p. 40)

The university education for this diverse intake was designed to be as broad as possible. Science students had to also take up some arts subjects in their first year. Students of the humanities studied one unit of science. Young people arriving at BU found themselves, as Baramki puts it, 'not only preparing for a degree but also engaging with wider questions' (p. 40):

> Since we felt certain we would have a state of our own very soon, we also emphasised the importance of democracy. Students learnt to value freedom of speech, but also that this did not mean you could insult or libel people. There had to be limits. Students had a chance to practice democracy in the student union. Everybody there had a right to be listened to, there were free elections and, while factions did gradually form, they had to resolve their differences by non-violent means. At Birzeit, there would be no weapons. Disagreements had to be resolved by dialogue. (p. 41)

This emphasis on the importance of democracy and dialogue – highlighted in the statement that heads this chapter – was and is maintained in a context of persistent oppression:

> Israel had no compunction about using torture on a huge scale. Palestinians under interrogation have been clubbed, hung by their arms for days, immersed in sewage, burnt and given repeated electric shocks to all parts of the body, including the genitals. Even more brutal methods were devised to extract names from the young detainees. And, once alleged student leaders had been identified, they would be tortured in turn to find out when they planned to demonstrate again or to stone Israeli soldiers. (p. 99)

One such student, Muhammed Shtayyeh, who had been detained on 1 January 1977 by a group of soldiers because he was carrying textbooks, was beaten unconscious, subsequently rearrested, held in detention for 116 days altogether (with 55 days of continuous torture and 65 in solitary confinement). As a direct result of the torture inflicted upon him, he was permanently disabled. He went on to gain a PhD and in 1991 was the first Palestinian to land in Madrid for the peace talks with Israel. He is now the Director General of the Palestinian Economic Council for Development and Reconstruction, a founding member of the Palestinian Development Fund and a trustee of Middle East Nonviolence and Democracy and of the Palestinian Center for Policy and Survey Research.

The erosion of freedom is, as Vally (2010) points out, relentless and impacts on academics and students alike:

> Palestinian academics daily run a gauntlet of soldiers, checkpoints, roadblocks, and the threat of arrest, detention and death in order to be able to get to their institutions to perform basic tasks like teaching and researching. They often teach classes that are sparsely populated usually because students could not get through the checkpoints. Students are sometimes trapped in their universities for days, unable to get home because of curfews and checkpoints. (p. 3)

Baramki (2010) insists on the importance of the ongoing struggle for freedom and democracy in the development of BU: 'while we are not yet free, we have always been able to teach our students about the key element in freedom, which is democracy. Democratic values were something that we tried to inculcate in students through university practices from the start'.

He insists, also, on the importance of mutual understanding and inter-connectivity and on the tragic consequences of failing to understand and to inter-connect:

> In order to resolve the conflict, some of us have tried to learn more about Jews and about Israelis. Many of us know about the holocaust; we can grasp its effects even on those Jews who did not actually suffer it, in the fear that some of them feel about a recurrence in the future. . . There seems to be no awareness that every tortured individual, every parent who loses a child, every child deprived of a parent, suffers in exactly the same way. (p. 161)

A Futures Curriculum

Human life is narrative in form: each of us is a unique trajectory. We are creatures in and of time. What we share – and what defines our commonality – is the experience of becoming uniquely ourselves, uniquely individualized, that is the paradox that informs and structures the human narrative. The precise course of any individual trajectory cannot be predetermined because it both acts upon and is responsive to the trajectories of others. The outcomes of individual actions cannot be pre-specified with complete certainty. To live a life entirely devoid of human unpredictability would be to have no life at all. We may seek to minimize the risk of the unpredictable through the exercise of wise choice, deliberation and circumspection, but the unpredictable – and therefore the un-pre-specifiable – is nevertheless always with us.

That is why, for example, Arendt (as quoted in Chapter 4) insists on 'a new kind of thinking that needs no pillars and props' and why Said insists upon reading Conrad's *Heart of Darkness* forward from the perspective of its late nineteenth century author rather than backwards from the retrospective viewpoint of its late twentieth or early twenty-first century critics. Our ontology as creatures of a particular time determines our hermeneutics: past and future can only be understood on their own terms which are entirely different from the terms in which we experience the present. We cannot unlearn what life has taught us. We cannot entirely undo what we have done and what others have done. We cannot perform a backward somersault into what we once were. As Isaiah Berlin (1996) famously remarked, 'the oak cannot return to the condition of the acorn'.

The cost of our flourishing as human agents is the irreversibility of the consequences that necessarily flow from our actions. This is one of the reasons why Nussbaum was concerned with 'the fragility of goodness' – the way in which goodness is always vulnerable to contingency and indeterminacy, to the forward movement of events and human actions and why, in all his varied body of work – art, criticism, film, documentary, novels, photography – Berger tells stories in which lives are seen to unfold and interact. There is, suggest Berger and Nussbaum, something irrevocable about our ways of doing and our ways of seeing. Both have irreversible consequences, the full import of which cannot be known in advance of the doing and the seeing. Of course, we seek to make sense of our lives in retrospect, but our lives can only be lived in prospect. We cannot live our lives in hindsight. The stories we tell ourselves about the past are not the stories we could have told ourselves about the future – for the simple reason that we did not know then what we know now. This is not just a matter of balancing risk on a scale of probability, but acknowledging the uncertainty of all human life: the fact that life provides us with neither the answers nor indeed the questions in advance. That is not to say that we can jettison all the old questions and answers, but that they can at best point us in the direction of whatever new questions and answers emerge. Learning is lifelong not by choice, but of necessity.

Any pedagogy that is sensitive to this ontological insight must acknowledge that at least some of the most significant outcomes of some of the most significant areas of human understanding cannot be pre-specified. They rely, that is, upon judgement, taste and discrimination, and what might be described as connoisseurship: qualities that we associate with interpretation. These areas of human understanding are traditionally associated with the arts and humanities, but in the increasingly mixed economy of human learning they now have a major contribution to make across the higher education curriculum. Technology, for example, is concerned with application – and application necessarily involves issues of value that require judgement, discrimination and connoisseurship. Insofar as higher education is concerned with the advancement of technology, it cannot overlook the ethical issues associated with the application of new technologies – or the cultural factors that frame those issues. Technology involves not just the acquisition of particular techniques, but the acquisition of those capabilities and dispositions necessary in the application of those techniques.

We cannot pre-specify for future generations what questions they will need to address or what knowledge and information they will require in order to address the unforeseeable question that will inevitably confront them. Yet our entire system of higher education is based on the assumption that this is precisely what we can and should be doing. Pedagogical competence and assessment criteria are defined on the bizarre assumption that teachers know what their students will learn before they have learnt it and that the academic achievement of those students can be assessed on that basis. An entire sector-wide industry comprising layer upon layer of bureaucratic and managerial excess has been built on the assumption that 'quality assurance' can somehow be safeguarded through the pre-specification of endless goals and targets and the measurement of outcomes in relation to those prior specifications – as if higher education were a production line and pedagogy the means of production.

Elsewhere I have termed the kind of curriculum that might result from this particular educational perspective as 'a futures curriculum' (Nixon, 2011a, 129–32). Such a curriculum would allow for some degree of specialization, but within a broad and balanced framework of provision that would allow for informed choice and, crucially, movement across the traditional divides of arts, humanities and sciences. It would encourage thinking across those boundaries – 'thinking without banisters' – while developing the capabilities and dispositions necessary for students to interpret the world and exercise their agency within it. It would rely on formative and developmental modes of assessment that would enable students to make informed judgements regarding their own aptitudes and interests. The criteria of assessment would be negotiated with individual students with reference to their prior choices and with a view to informing their future choices.

A futures curriculum for higher education would, in other words, require a bolder and riskier mediation between the claims of established specialist areas and those of new and emergent fields of study. It would provide students with the resources necessary to become flexible in their crossing of intellectual boundaries, open and receptive to new ideas and practices, collaborative and confident in working with others and capable of seeing their own area of specialist expertise in a wider context. This can only be achieved by broadening the base of curriculum provision and ensuring that all students are exposed to a range of ideas and viewpoints, to different modes of thinking and understanding, and to a variety of communicative and discursive forms. Isolated initiatives, however innovative they may be, are not sufficient. Institutions will need to address the issue holistically and build a shared understanding across all members of faculty that this is the way forward into the future.

These institution-wide reforms refuse any easy dichotomy between 'depth' and 'breadth'. They acknowledge that in an increasingly interconnected world, 'breadth' is itself a constituent of the 'depth' dimension. The ability to locate and relocate specialist knowledge and expertise in a variety of contexts – to be creative in its application and imaginative in its potential for transfer – will become increasingly valuable in a rapidly changing world. Similarly, the need for flexibility in course provision and in the accreditation of diverse achievements – at different levels of achievement – will be essential if higher education is to meet the needs and expectations of future generations of students. The idea that 'breadth' dilutes or compromises 'depth' of study must be challenged not just on pragmatic grounds but on epistemological grounds. A futures curriculum has at its core a notion of knowledge as infinitely inter-connective and endlessly and unpredictably engaging.

Becoming Ourselves

Learning individualizes us and enables us to become ourselves through the clarification of our interests and the development of our particular aptitudes and capabilities. Education can either acknowledge the individualizing dynamic of human understanding and thereby focus on individual self-development and flourishing, or it can insist upon conformity and homogeneity and in so doing restrict and constrain that dynamic. That tension is present in any education system, since, as we saw in Chapter 2, education has developed historically as a means of both state control and individual emancipation – a means of controlling 'the masses' and of remaking 'the public'. The pedagogical point at issue is how to ensure that education inflects towards the latter – how, that is, to ensure equality, not through the imposition of sameness and conformity, but by encouraging the unique human potential of each individual.

For Arendt, that issue focuses on the relation between thought and action. Thinking, she maintained, is not in itself an action, but provides the conditions necessary for right action or at least for avoiding wrong action or inaction. To fail to think is to risk becoming an unthinking cog in a machine – a mechanistic operative for whom routine behaviour takes the place of moral agency. The amoral endpoint of this process is what she termed 'the banality of evil' and saw exemplified in the person of Eichmann. Becoming thoughtful was for Arendt a moral imperative. Berger sees a similar imperative attached to the process of becoming attentive. The content of that to which we are giving our attention cannot be defined solely in terms of its subject matter, since it is constituted in part also by the particular perspective we adopt. Moreover, we must take responsibility not only for what we choose to attend to, but also for the perspective we adopt in relation to it.

By becoming attentive we not only see the object more clearly and in all its distinctiveness, but we also define ourselves in relation to that object.

All understanding is necessarily reflexive and self-defining. In the process of interpreting the world, we locate the interpretive self within that world. This insight is central to Said's insistence on the complementarity of reception and critique in any act of interpretation. Criticism, for Said, is only as good as the understanding that informs it. We define our critical selves – and develop our critical faculties – through a disciplined process of scholarly receptivity. We cannot usefully criticize until we understand what it is we are criticizing and we cannot understand what it is we are criticizing without some sense of our own critical distance from it. That is the guiding principle of 'philological hermeneutics' as Said sought to practice it: seek to understand the part (in all its complex detail) in relation to the whole (in its complex entirety) before trusting to one's own independent judgement. That is why Said insisted that criticism is humanistic, secular and democratic – it is, even at its most severe, rooted in the desire for mutual understanding.

In her insistence on the universal significance of the capabilities of practical reasoning and affiliation, Nussbaum places a similar emphasis on becoming oneself within the context of other people becoming themselves. We learn to reason together only by virtue of our being able to live together. Respect for our own and others' freedom of choice is, as we saw in Chapter 7, all important for Nussbaum in achieving the capabilities necessary for human development. Only when we freely choose to fulfil our potential can we be said to have achieved capability. Pedagogy, then, is not simply a matter of providing opportunities for learning, but also a matter of ensuring that those who are provided with those opportunities have the freedom to take them or reject them. Choice is what transforms capacity into capability. Pedagogy, insofar as it is concerned with that process of transformation, is necessarily involved in the mediation and negotiation of choice: enabling students to understand the implications of the choices that are open to them and the implications of the choices that they make – enabling them, that is, to become themselves.

A 'futures curriculum' would provide the flexibility and guidance necessary for students to become themselves in this way. This has implications for the structure of the higher education curriculum and for the organization of the curriculum as a whole, particularly in relation to entry and exit routes and for the recognition of different levels of achievement. Finally, it has implications for how the idea of becoming an 'independent learner' is embedded within pedagogic practice.

A Joined-up Curriculum

The higher education curriculum has become increasingly fragmented to the extent that any notion of 'a whole curriculum' or 'a common curriculum' is virtually meaningless. Even within particular disciplines of study, it may be difficult to conceive of an integrated curriculum within which students have a shared experience of learning. Modular frameworks which address this problem at the systemic level may exacerbate it at the experiential level – with both students and teachers failing to grasp the supposed interconnectivity of the modular structure. The desired coherence thereby dissipates into a sense of discontinuity. This increasing specialization aims at increased student autonomy through the exercise of choice and the provision of alternative pathways. In reality, however, it can diminish that autonomy by prematurely closing down options before students have had the opportunity to fully grasp the implications of the choices they are making.

We become ourselves as learners by understanding the kinds of learners we want to be. Within the current system, that is very difficult. A student gains admission to a university to study a particular course on the basis of an already specialized programme of study in the final years of schooling. Having been accepted onto that course there are likely to be optional elements, but only within the prescribed framework of that discipline or field of study. There is unlikely to be significant interchange between the arts, sciences and humanities, unless the student is registered on the kind of programme routinely dismissed by tabloids and politicians as leading to a 'mickey mouse degree'. We need a broader and more balanced curriculum at the level of undergraduate study in order to ensure that all students have access to different modes of understanding. We also need much greater flexibility so that students can move across academic divides and boundaries – including institutional divides and boundaries. All undergraduate students should be pursuing programmes of study that open their minds to the full possibilities of human understanding: the wonders of science, the delights of mathematics, the disciplines of the various arts and the wisdom of the humanities.

Exits and Entrances

If we need to regain a sense of the whole curriculum that introduces students to the full span of human understanding, we also need to regain for all students a sense of achievement and progress. Currently, students who for whatever reason do not complete a course of undergraduate study almost invariably are deemed to have failed or, in exceptional cases, to have interrupted their studies. Such students are given no public recognition for the work they have undertaken or indeed for the hard and difficult decision they may have taken in discontinuing their study. The experience of higher education for such students is likely to be one of failure and a source of continuing resentment. Universities that cater predominantly for first-generation students and students from economically disadvantaged backgrounds have a disproportionate number of such students. Far from helping these students to become themselves – to become confident members of society and active citizens within the polity – the higher education system identifies them as 'failures', 'drop-outs', 'non-completers'.

The real failure, however, lies in the system itself: its failure to re-route students according to their interests and needs, its failure to link across departments and institutions, its failure to recognize the individual needs and aspirations of students. Institutions of higher education are trapped into a system of competitive isolation which renders them incapable of responding cooperatively to the needs of individual students. Cities of little more than half a million inhabitants can boast that they host two or even three major universities, none of which collaborate at the level of student learning and all of which are in competition with one another for funding and for prestige. We need a system that recognizes achievement, promotes the interests of students rather than the self-interest of institutions, provides flexibility of entry and exit across institutions and demands cross-institutional collaboration.

Interdependencies

Such a system would require a new kind of academic professionalism defined in terms of the values and the practices associated with interdependency: the values of mutuality and recognition and the practices of collaboration and negotiation. In particular, the notion of 'independent learning' would require careful attention. None of us is fully independent in our attempts to understand the world and our relation to that world. We are crucially dependent on the insights of others. No one who seriously wants to understand can possibly claim to be wholly independent. Pedagogy begins with the central insight that understanding involves interdependency. It is dialogical. Independence within the context of human understanding is a process, not an achieved state. Dante found an archetypal metaphor for the interdependency of human learning when in the opening canto of *The Divine Comedy* he introduces Virgil as the one who will guide him through the circles of hell and purgatory to Beatrice who will lead him through to paradise. In order to achieve the supreme understanding as expressed in the final canto of that epic, Dante must be led every step of the way by those whom he trusts and to whom he has been entrusted.

In contrast, contemporary Western culture places a premium on independence and autonomy, to the extent that any acknowledgement of need can be viewed negatively. Criticism of 'the welfare state' is very often couched in precisely these terms, whereby need is seen as reprehensible and those who are in need are labelled as 'scroungers'. In higher education not wholly dissimilar arguments are sometimes used by those who criticize colleagues for creating a dependency culture among students and treating higher education as a form of emotional therapy. Few would disagree that enforced dependency is wrong and that treating higher education as anything other than education is undesirable. However, the criticism is entirely misplaced. Students are not suffering from a surfeit of attention. Their concerns as expressed in countless student surveys focus on lack of information at the point of entry, lack of contact time with tutors and lack of adequate and helpful feedback. Students do not become independent learners by being treated as if they were already independent learners. They become independent by learning how to operate within – and take full advantage of – the multiple interdependencies that are involved in all learning at whatever level.

Pedagogy as Quest

Berger (1992) opens his trilogy of novels, *Into Their Labours*, with a question about the content of the many stories that are woven into the complex narrative pattern of this work. 'We must now ask this question' he insists: 'what is the contemporary relation between peasants and the world economic system of which they form a part? Or, to put this question in terms of our consideration of peasant experience: What significance can this experience have today in a global context?' (p. xxv). We see here, also, the refinement of 'this question' whereby Berger feels the need to focus it specifically on 'our consideration of peasant experience'. Between the two formulations of the question lies the moral project of the entire trilogy: how to shift our perspective in such a way that the 'peasant experience' becomes the prime focus of our reading of this great work of narrative art. This shift is precisely what pedagogy would be seeking to occasion under these circumstances – a shift that denotes a realignment of perspective and subject such that the content of, in this case, a trilogy of interwoven stories is brought into sharp focus.

We become ourselves – open up the future to ourselves and ourselves to the future – through a pedagogic process that is social and interactive and at the same time individualizing and formative. Interdependence and the individuation are two of the defining features of this process. A third defining feature relates directly to the purposefulness of that process: the purpose of pedagogy is to enhance understanding; the purpose of understanding is to formulate meaningful questions; and the purpose of meaningful questions is to further enhance our shared understanding. The purposefulness of the pedagogic process resides, in other words, in its capacity to generate meaningful questions: questions that challenge the *status quo* while being comprehensible within whatever constitutes that *status quo*. Meaningful questions rattle the cage of meaning – they point us in the direction of what cannot be made explicit, but can be shown: 'what *can* be shown, *cannot* be said' was how Wittgenstein (2001, p. 31) put it.

Whose Questions?

Higher education tends to define students as respondents to already formulated questions. Their lecturers pose questions to which they invariably know the answer and students are assessed on their ability to respond intelligently (i.e. in an informed and appropriate manner) to these questions. Bright students reflect back to their lecturers what those lecturers already know and very bright students occasionally risk taking their lecturers by surprise and providing them with information or insights that are beyond the remit of the question. Students become adept at responding to questions, the answers to which their lecturers (who are almost always the people assessing them) have already formulated. Indeed, the academic authority of their lecturers – the prime reason they were appointed to their posts – is that they can provide an expert answer to the questions posed by their students.

Holly Smith (2008, 715), an academic working within the higher education sector of the UK, explains the implications of this tired pedagogical routine whereby lecturers ask questions, the answer to which they already know. She sees it as a power game tilted against the educational interests of the students:

> In a world where there are right answers and only the teacher knows them, all assessment must seem a cruel joke where the natural order is reversed and the omniscient ask the ignorant for answers. . . Students'

natural anxiety to succeed (under the pressure of tuition fees, debts and combining paid work with study) will lead them, as it would any rational person, to do that which is rewarded.

Of course, good teachers have always shown their students how to pose questions and how to address those same questions, but that is very different from telling their students what questions to address and the terms within which to address them. Arendt knew how to sharpen her questioning through making distinctions. As Kohn, quoted in Chapter 4, points out, her thinking found its focus through a process of careful discrimination: 'A is not B, totalitarianism is not tyranny, force is not power, action is not work, work is not labour, the private is not public, thinking is not willing, willing is not judging, sympathy is not compassion and compassion is not empathy ('I' am not 'Thou')'. (Young-Bruehl and Kohn, 2001, 242–3). It was that mode of questioning through the making of distinctions that was Arendt's legacy to her students. She undoubtedly questioned them, but primarily she provided them with a model of how to question.

The crucial questions are not those posed by the teacher, but those formulated by the students. Many teachers who pride themselves on their use of 'the Socratic method' to question their students lose sight of the fundamental Socratic insight that students must themselves become questioners as well as respondents. Good teachers may model that process – the lecture form can, for example, be used to show how the lecturer thinks within the framework of her or his area of study – but for students to fully engage with that area of study they must formulate the questions that make it relevant to their own concerns and circumstances. That is why (as discussed in Chapter 7), Nussbaum insists on the importance of volition and choice in the formation of human capabilities. We become 'capable' by engaging our capacities and potentialities – by realizing them – and by rendering them relevant to our needs and aspirations.

How we question what we receive – particularly when what we receive is deemed canonical within our discipline or field of study – is crucial to this process of engagement. What we receive originated as a response to earlier sets of questions and can only be understood in that historical context. Our questioning of what we receive will, in turn, prompt new questions. To enter this process of question and answer is to enter a conversation, the purpose of which is to develop our understanding. In entering that conversation, we enter history. It is the role of the teacher always to facilitate that entry and thereby ensure the sustainability of the conversation.

Question and Answer

Within the context of higher education, the role that teachers play in this process is crucial. Questions, for example, need to be meaningful in the context within which they are posed and addressed – they are the means by which we enter into an ongoing conversation. They also presuppose prior and subsequent questions – questions differ and require ordering and sequencing. Working one's way through this complex process is the stuff of scholarship and studentship. To be a student is to begin to negotiate this field. The teacher helps in this task of negotiation by modelling the questioning, encouraging the questioner, helping to frame and contextualize the questions, acting as an initial respondent, etc. However, the questions must belong to the student – and must be framed within a context that encourages and supports the student as questioner. We develop our understanding through the formulation and refinement of questions.

The surest guide to the pedagogical implications of this claim is the philosopher, historian and archaeologist, R.G. Collingwood (see Inglis, 2009). The fifth chapter of Collingwood's autobiography (first published in 1939) is devoted to what he terms 'question and answer' – or 'the "questioning activity" in knowledge' (Collingwood, 1978, 29–43). His awareness of the importance of the 'logic of question and answer' developed gradually through his vast range of scholarly interests (philosophy, art, history. . .) and hobbies (archaeology, music, sailing. . .):

> I began by observing that you cannot find out what a man means by simply studying his spoken or written statements, even though he has spoken or written with perfect command of language and perfectly truthful intention. In order to find out his meaning you must also know what the question was (a question in his own mind, and presumed by him to be in yours) to which the thing he has said or written was meant as an answer. (p. 31)

Question and answer, he maintained, are 'strictly correlative'. An answer could only be 'right' in relation to the specific question being addressed. Moreover, the detail and particularity of the question had to match the detail and particularity of the answer. To illustrate this point, he takes the example of his car failing to start and his spending an hour searching for the cause of the failure:

> If, during this hour, I take out number one plug, lay it on the engine, turn the starting-handle, and watch for a spark, my observation 'number one

> plug is all right' is an answer not to the question, 'Why won't my car go?' but to the question, 'Is it because number one plug is not sparking that my car won't go?' (p. 32)

He goes on to argue that any one of the various experiments he might make during the hour would be the finding of an answer to some detailed and particularized question and would contribute to 'the logic of question and answer' – the cumulative 'complex consisting of questions and answers':

> The question, 'Why won't my car go?' is only a kind of summary of all these taken together. It is not a separate question asked at a separate time, nor is it a sustained question which I continue to ask for the whole hour together. Consequently, when I say 'Number one plug is all right', this observation does not record one more failure to answer the hour-long question, What is wrong with my car?' It records a success in answering the three-minute-long question, 'Is the stoppage due to failure in number one plug?'

Collingwood shows how this process of deliberative reasoning through question and answer is deeply pedagogical. It is not only something we all to a greater or lesser extent learn, but also something that can be taught: how to correlate question and answer, how to sequence and order questions, how to interpret statements, propositions, texts, etc. with reference to the 'question-and-answer complex' within which they were originally located.

***

Pedagogy must be viewed as part of an institution-wide orientation towards cross-institutional collaboration and partnership: the pedagogicized university. For national regions such as the UK, with a long history of deepening stratification across its higher education system, this may well sound retrograde or utopian. For institutions such as the University of Birzeit, it is a necessary condition of survival. Within the context of a global economic crisis which the West is manifestly incapable of managing and containing – witness the social consequences of that crisis which are erupting onto the streets and public places of the urbanized West – the re-envisioning of pedagogy and its civic bases is far from retrograde or utopian. It is a necessity. Institutions of higher education must become more pedagogical in their internal organization and ethos and in their outreach; the higher education sector must become more coordinated and joined-up across its traditionally competitive institutional boundaries; and national systems must become more open and flexible in terms of transfer and permeability across nation states. Pedagogy, in other words, needs to be defined within a broader context of institutional and civic interconnectivity.

Chapter 9

Educated Publics

Positioned within these geopolitical crossroads . . .

(Anatoly Oleksiyenko, 2012, forthcoming)

Pedagogic practice finds its moral endpoint in the public sphere – in the constitution of an educated public comprising 'citizens of the world'. This view is, of course, seriously at odds with the dominant view of both pedagogic practice (something that academics do in lecture halls, seminar rooms and occasionally in tutorials) and professional ethics (codes of conduct governing the behaviour of individual academics). Although there has been a sustained focus of interest over the last thirty years in 'professional ethics' and 'ethical practice', that focus has tended to employ a narrow lens through which ethics is viewed as professional accountability and professionalism is viewed as a kind of ethical checklist. Indeed, 'professional ethics' has become fully 'professionalized' with its own officialize, its own organizational structures, its own experts and – inevitably – its own input into professionally and vocationally oriented courses and modules. Ethics has become professionalized, professions have become institutionalized and institutions have become increasingly inward-looking and self-interested in their relentless drive for the competitive cutting edge. We need to look beyond our own boundaries for transformational possibilities.

Prologue: Cross-border Transformations

The University of Central Asia (UCA) was founded in 2000 by the governments of Kazakhstan, Kyrgyzstan and Tajikistan and His Highness the Aga Khan (the 49th hereditary Imam and spiritual leader of the Shia Ismaili Muslim community). It is a private, independent, self-governing institution and the world's first internationally chartered institution of higher education. The governments of Kazakhstan, Kyrgyzstan and Tajikistan have all contributed land and other benefits and the Aga Khan has contributed a substantial endowment fund. Funding also comes from international donor agencies, governments, foundations, corporations and individuals. Students are expected to contribute to the cost of their education, but no qualified student is denied entry for financial reasons. Financial aid is available in the form of scholarships, grants, loans and work–study programmes.

Launched amidst the dramatic political, social and economic transformations of the post-Soviet period, the UCA had, as Anatoly Oleksiyenko (2012, forthcoming) points out, to give a substantial amount of thought to its start-up strategy:

> Within the post-colonial context, shaped by the frantic competition of ideas and symbols propelled by globalisation, the university had to consider three major challenges: 1) how to prevent a reversal to the old Soviet template of higher education, 2) how to avoid the blind-copying or borrowing of western models, and 3) how to create an original local model that would make it possible to overcome the peripheral standing of Central Asia's higher education systems.

In addition, there are considerable socio-economic disparities between the three participating states. Tajikistan has suffered ethnic conflict and civil war since the collapse of the Soviet Union and has been struggling to reconfigure its economy. This task of reconfiguration is further complicated by the fact that 90 per cent of Tajikistan's territory is taken up by mountain ranges and that access to remote populations is therefore difficult. Given its relatively stronger economic position, the government of Kazakhstan has been able to allocate annually 3000 scholarships to Kazakh students to study at overseas universities. Neither Kyrgyzstan nor Tajikistan has sufficient means for such allocations. Clearly, the asymmetries inside the alliance, as well as in the larger geopolitical architecture, are quite significant. 'Positioned within these geopolitical crossroads', argues Oleksiyenko, 'the Central Asian countries need to perform a delicate balancing act in order to pursue and maintain their own economic and political interests and mitigate lingering instability'.

Within this context, the UCA has emerged as a strategic partnership, the prime purpose of which is to promote the socio-economic development of Central Asia's predominantly rural and economically disadvantaged mountain societies. As Oleksiyenko points out, the relation between the three participating national regions is vital: 'partnership is conceptualized as a mutually beneficial framework, both on paper and on the ground'. It is important in this respect that the three university campuses – located in Khorog (Tajikistan), Tekeli (Kazakhstan) and Naryn (Kyrgyzstan) – share equal status within the partnership. It is also important, given the purpose of the partnership that these locations are all small towns situated in poor mountainous areas but within commuting distance to the capital cities of their respective countries. Finally, it is important for the sustainability of the partnership that the university is a secular institution espousing no religion or creed and with an international outreach facilitated in part by the existing global networks established through the Aga Khan Development Network.

The undergraduate curriculum blends what the UCA calls 'general humanistic and scientific education with one that offers marketable skills'. A core curriculum taken throughout the first two years introduces all students to 'modes of thought and methods of inquiry in the humanities, social sciences and sciences'. This core element includes 'teaching of ethics across the curriculum to support the moral reasoning students need to become responsible, compassionate and active civic-minded members of society'. The undergraduate programme as a whole seeks to foster 'a research-oriented education culture by having students engage in original research projects starting in their second year'. In recognition of the diversity of student intake and the disadvantaged backgrounds from which many of the students are drawn, a one-year undergraduate preparatory programme and a three-month graduate preparatory programme are provided for students entering UCA (www.ucentralasia.org/programmes.asp).

In addition, UCA's School of Professional and Continuing Education is providing courses in a range of certificated courses across its national regions. These courses are linking with institutions throughout Central Asia, Egypt and Pakistan in an attempt to meet the professional and vocational needs of the local, regional, national and international economies. This global, national and local interconnectivity – at the level of pedagogy and curriculum – is vital to the sustainability of UCA:

> UCA has developed vibrant links in areas such as natural resource management, business and economic development, tourism, education policy and public management, among others, with well-established schools in Europe and Asia, which offer support in terms of program accreditation, doctoral fellowships, visiting professorships, faculty and student exchange, and joint 'research for development'. The joint projects developed with these international partners have a clear focus on local capacity-building. Academic programmes address the immediate needs of small towns and

> villages in the region. In addition to economic objectives, the development of resources for local folklore, music and humanities projects is part of major interdisciplinary endeavours receiving the UCA's support and attention. (Oleksiyenko, 2012, forthcoming)

UCA is attempting to connect its pedagogic practice not only across its unique framework of international governance, but also more widely. It has no option. It must reach out locally, nationally and globally or fail to survive. Reaching out is not an optional extra for UCA – or even a moral imperative – but a necessary condition of sustainability. It cannot afford the privilege of insularity.

De-professionalizing Ethics

It is not insignificant that the rise of 'professional ethics' within the UK and more generally in the West coincided with, on the one hand, the erosion of the public sector and the demise of the public sector professional and, on the other hand, the expansion of the private sector and the emergence of the private sector professional as the model of the new public management. In the new world of public accountability, target-setting and managerial efficiency, what was going to take the place of the good old-fashioned public service ethic? How, given that professional practitioners were no longer to be trusted but endlessly audited by a class of super-professional managers, could those practitioners be persuaded to take professional responsibility for their own professional practice? How could post-welfare regimes command the support of their 'public servants'?

The emphasis on 'professional ethics' and 'ethical practice' provided a partial answer to these kinds of questions. Professional ethics could, after all, be managed; it could be bureaucratized; it could be absorbed into existing systems of accountability. It could also be individualized. It could shift responsibility for the ethical conduct of professional practice onto the individual professional and leave the corporate state, and the corporate institutions supported by such a state, free to get on with their core business: making a profit. As privatization became the *sine qua non* of institutional efficiency, so individualization became the guiding principle of ethical practice. Institutions would take responsibility for determining the right thing to do, while professionals would work out the right way of doing it; or, to use the jargon, institutions would take responsibility for 'strategic planning' and professional practitioners would take responsibility for, and be held accountable for, implementing such plans 'efficiently' and 'cost effectively'.

Within higher education, this strategy has proved remarkably successful as a managerial ploy. It has also inflicted untold harm on institutions of higher education and on the professionals who maintain the practices that are integral to those institutions. Institutions have, in effect, outsourced their ethical responsibilities to an academic work force that is increasingly powerless to speak back with moral authority to those institutions. Academics, for example, regularly decry research assessment and teaching quality audit exercises which consume vast resources and provide little or no formative and developmental feedback. Those same academics, however, routinely service those exercises, by, for example, sitting on panels and providing 'expert' advice; very often they gain professional prestige and preferment for doing so as well as financial remuneration. At the same time, many of them jealously guard what they term their 'academic autonomy' and uphold their self-declared right to 'academic freedom'.

As Simon Head (Associate Fellow at the Rothermere American Institute at Oxford and a Scholar at the Institute for Public Knowledge at New York University) points out: 'with the recession eating away at the budgets of universities on both sides of the Atlantic, the times are not propitious for those hoping to liberate scholarship and teaching from harmful managerial schemes'. Such liberation, he argues, would require 'a stronger and better-organized resistance on the part of the academy itself than we have seen so far' (Simon Head, 2011, 64). Indeed, one might argue that such resistance constitutes a moral imperative for all professional academics working within higher education: the moral necessity, that is, of challenging, in the name of their own academic professionalism, all such 'harmful managerial schemes'. It is, ironically, their own collusion in the bureaucratization of professional ethics that prevents most academic professionals most of the time from taking such an ethical stance.

Institutional Ethos

If we are to consider professional ethics in relation to pedagogic practice, we must focus primarily on institutional context. We must then acknowledge that the context is constitutive of the ethics. Institutions cannot lay the ethical burden exclusively on the individual professional; nor can individuals off-load their ethical responsibilities onto the institution; ethics is centrally concerned with mutuality and interdependence. Nevertheless, within the current context, the reduction of the ethical to an individualist rather than associative category is particularly marked. The moral hazard comes in the main not from the professional ethics of the individual practitioner, but from the institutional ethos within which practitioners operate. We need to focus both on the ethics of the professional situated within the institution and on the ethos of the institution located within the broader frame of civil society.

The field of academic practice is characterized by increasing specialization and diversification. Within both the UK and the US, the higher education sector has become deeply divided, with a small minority of institutions gaining the majority of research funds (and thereby consolidating their premier league status as 'research-led' institutions) and with the large majority of institutions defining themselves as 'teaching-led' (and thereby acknowledging their relegation to the second league). This state of affairs is, of course, defended on the basis of diversity and the maximization of choice. In reality, however, the insistence on choice and diversity masks inequalities in relation to access to and participation in higher education. As shown in the ongoing work of the Sutton Trust cited in Chapter 1, the premier league universities not only cater for a disproportionate number of students who have benefited from private education, but also supply the highest paid professions with a disproportionate number of their senior and most highly paid personnel.

This stratification of the higher education sector has led to the increased atomization of academic professionalism. Institutions routinely rely on part-time staff, fixed-term contracts and teaching only contracts in order to retain maximum control of the workforce and to ensure that they retain staff with the greatest 'prestige' value. Since 'prestige' is invariably associated with research output, the most vulnerable members of the academic community are likely to be those whose contracts carry a heavy teaching load and who may be given little or no time to develop their own research profiles. Many institutions require doctoral students and post-doctoral fellows to carry a heavy teaching load, with the result that they are poorly placed to develop their research interests and build a serious publications list. It takes at least eleven years of full-time schooling, at least three years of full-time undergraduate study, usually one year of full-time study at masters level and at least three years of full-time doctoral study to prepare someone just to begin a career as an academic. Many institutions of higher education then routinely squander that precious resource by relegating newly appointed staff to short, fixed-term contracts that allow little or no time for research and are designed to relieve more senior staff of their teaching responsibilities.

Even among professorial staff with international reputations, the inequalities are huge though often masked. It is not uncommon in research-led institutions for the most highly paid professors to be paid twice as much as their professorial peers, on the basis of the research income they bring to the institution, the supposed prestige of their research outputs and the nature of their subject specialism. In effect it means that the most highly paid members of academic staff are likely to be doing the least teaching and are least likely to be in regular contact with undergraduate students. They are also most likely to have access to additional funding that allows them, for example, to attend overseas conferences, establish research initiatives and research scholarships and, crucially, buy themselves out of the routine teaching duties. Such entrenched hierarchies have the effect of clogging the system and preventing career mobility and advancement particularly for young academics on the lower rungs of the promotional ladder.

The increase in the financial remuneration of vice chancellors and principals – across the higher education sector – at a time when redundancies and redeployment of academic staff is the order of the day – shows a lack of sensitivity by those in receipt of these remuneration packages and their governing councils coupled with a lack of moral authority and intellectual leadership. The point that has to be acknowledged in any serious debate on professional ethics – as it relates to institutions of higher education – is that the financial remuneration of the supposed leaders of those institutions deeply affects the ethos of those institutions. Vice chancellors and principals and their spokespersons may seek to justify these huge increases, but the crucial question for the purposes of this argument is whether or not they can do so on moral grounds. I can think of no moral justification for vice chancellors and principals receiving, in some cases, a twenty per cent increase (and over) at a time when lecturers' salaries are falling in real terms and those same vice chancellors and principles are arguing publicly that institutional sustainability depends upon financial stringency and staff cuts.

One has to add to this somewhat bizarre working environment an administrative cadre that notwithstanding its own internal inequalities has contributed hugely to the general marginalization of academic influence and professional judgement within institutions of higher education. Senior management teams of institutions of higher education – that is, those with overall responsibility for the strategic development of the institution as a whole – are now routinely staffed by administrators who may well outnumber academics. Head of department and of faculty – that is, those with strategic *and* operational responsibility for their particular units – are invariably seen as quasi-managers answerable to the administrative offices of the institution. In a situation of financial stringency, occasioned by huge cuts in public expenditure coupled with the semi-privatization of higher education, this over-reliance on the administrative and managerial cadre is a matter of public concern.

We risk losing the ethics of pedagogic practice in a brown fog of bureaucratic pedantry in which ethics becomes little more than a disconnected exercise in professional and institutional self-justification. We need, in short, an ethics of connectivity: an ethics centrally concerned with and orientated towards the sustainability of an educated public. This would be an ethics that looked to the future and took seriously the supremely important cross-generational aspects of human interconnectivity. However, in order to achieve any sense of what an ethics of connectivity might look like, we need to understand some of the main blockages that are currently preventing it – blockages that although systemic and structural are experienced as professional and sometimes deeply personal dilemmas by those working in higher education.

The Primacy of Practice

Current systems of accreditation, assessment and quality control routinely deny the epistemological assumptions upon which all teaching and learning is based. Courses are accredited, students are assessed and quality is supposedly maintained on the assumption that the outcomes of learning that can be pre-specified (and, more often than not, quantified) are the outcomes that are educationally worthwhile (i.e. noteworthy). It would be almost impossible to find a teacher who genuinely subscribes to the view that this is what constitutes higher education. As argued in the previous chapter, pedagogy is centrally concerned with the unpredictability of human understanding and with enabling students to ease their way forward into the unknown. The bureaucratic obsession with the pre-specification of learning outcomes excludes precisely those elements that are educationally worthwhile. The educational goods of learning – those goods that are, in other words, a defining characteristic of educational practice – are thereby denied by the very systems that are designed to sustain them.

This disparity between system and practice clearly presents the academic practitioner with dilemmas in her or his role as a teacher, since there is at the very least a tension and at worst a contradiction in the bureaucratic demands of the overlapping audit systems and the educational demands of educationally purposeful pedagogic practice. These dilemmas are compounded by the competing and sometimes incompatible policy agendas impacting upon academic practice. Academic practitioners traditionally fulfil triple responsibilities (and roles): a pedagogic responsibility for students (teaching role); a scholastic responsibility towards their general field of study or discipline (research role); and a collegial responsibility towards the intellectual community of their host institution (administrative role). Although new and emergent divisions of labour have 'unbundled' some of these roles and responsibilities and assigned them to different occupational groupings, most academics in most institutions continue to fulfil these various roles and responsibilities albeit in very different combinations. In doing so, they are obliged to meet the demands of different policy agendas emanating from different government departments and mediated through different administrative offices of their own institution.

In this clash of priorities, teaching has undoubtedly suffered. A survey conducted by the Open University Centre for Higher Education Research and Information found that between 1992 and 2007, there had been a decline in the number of hours academics reported spending on teaching and an increase in the amount of time UK academics reported spending on research. The proportion of academics that reported a primary interest in teaching had also decreased since 1992, while the percentage of staff claiming a primary interest in research rose by 9 per cent. Moreover, far fewer UK academics in the UK reported a primary interest in teaching compared with their international counterparts, with the UK lagging far behind China, South Africa and the USA (Universities UK, 2008). Clearly, the Research Assessment Exercise, which since 1986 had set the research agenda within higher education, was impacting much more forcefully on the professional identity of academics than the widening participation agenda, which since 1997 had set a 50 per cent participation target with a view to closing the social class gap (ESRC, 2008).

Systemic Clashes

This clash of priorities presents academics with complex ethical dilemmas. At one level, the choice (which will be largely determined by institutional context and prior career choices) is between teaching and research, each of which makes its distinct ethical claims. At the level of day-to-day practice, the choice may be more pressing: do I prioritize that recently convened research seminar over a prior tutorial commitment? Do I miss out on the former or re-schedule the latter? Do I prioritize the completion of the chapter and thereby meet the agreed deadline or do I provide full, detailed and prompt feedback on a student assignment that is particularly weak and in need of extensive revision? It is clear from the evidence available that these ethical choices are increasingly skewed towards the research priorities of the institution and away from the pedagogical priorities of the student experience of teaching and learning. Professional ethics are determined by an institutional ethos that is largely determined by sector-wide systems over which institutions have little influence and academics have little or no control. To turn the argument on its head in this way – calling to moral account the institution as well as the individual – is not to absolve academic practitioners of moral responsibility for their own practice, but to highlight the importance of institutional ethos as a necessary condition of professional ethics.

The disparity between system and practice also impacts on the field of academic research where it is experienced as value dissonance between the kinds of research practices that research councils say they are trying to promote and the systems of research assessment that are used to allocate resources. Thus, academics are encouraged to engage in collaborative, interdisciplinary and cross-institutional research, while operating within an assessment regime within which academic departments and institutions compete against one another for research funds. It is a self-perpetuating and stultifying system: those institutions that gained the higher levels of funding in the previous assessment round are best placed to gain even higher levels of funding in subsequent rounds, while those towards the bottom end of the research league tables lack the resources necessary to develop their research capacity. The latter might benefit hugely from involvement in cross-institutional programmes of work, but research-intensive institutions are unlikely to risk their competitive edge by entering into such collaborations. The sector, as a whole, thereby suffers. It is not just that some institutions lose out, but that the practice of research is distorted through the systematic denial of its collaborative potential.

Systemic Irrationality

Systems may be rational in the sense of being internally coherent, but wholly irrational in the sense of being disconnected from the practices they seek to sustain. Indeed, the over-rationalization of systems is very often an indicator of their irrationality in respect of practice. This irrationality has the effect of ensuring that practitioners are operating in a situation of chronic moral dilemma, since the goods of their particular practice are denied by the systems that exist to support them. This is undoubtedly the case in higher education where the problem has been exacerbated by the managers of such systems blaming practitioners for failing to ensure that their practices fully conform to what the practitioners see as inappropriate and therefore irrational systems. This problem can only be resolved by an institutional reorientation towards practice and through the development of systems that are respectful of – and true to – the logic of specific practices. Those practices carry their own particular goods, which provide them with their integrity and their logic. Systems relating to academic practice – and those who manage such systems – must understand that logic if they are to avoid putting those goods at risk.

This does not mean that we can or should do away with systems. We need systems, but we need better systems – complex systems with a capacity for adaptability, consultation, flexibility, negotiation, responsiveness, synthesis, etc. – and systems managers who understand the moral grammar of practice. In order to begin to think seriously about the ethics of academic professionalism, academics need a trusting – and trustworthy – environment in which an increasingly influential administrative cadre listen and learn. In particular, those who manage and administer institutional and sector-wide systems – finance and resourcing, corporate planning, external relations, quality assurance, etc. – need to be aware that practices have histories and that histories are embedded in traditions. The traditions, as I argued in Chapter 3, render the practices sustainable, while the practices ensure the continuity and openness of the traditions (see Gadamer, 2004; MacIntyre, 1985).

Systemic Time

Traditions carry tacit understandings and intuitive insights that are indispensable to the practitioner and that all practitioners must learn to trust (Polanyi, 1958; Polanyi and Prosch, 1975). Trusting to these insights and understandings is a defining characteristic of the mature practitioner. They provide the practitioner with an awareness of, among other things, the rhythms of the particular activity within which he or she is engaged. Tradition tells us that academic practice takes time and that the time taken is not easily amenable to pre-specification: re-thinking is central to thinking; drafting involves redrafting; clarity of perspective requires revision. Academic practice is an organic process, the rhythms of which must be acknowledged and respected. The organized time of institutions and of the systems that normalize and standardize institutional life beat to a different rhythm and a different pace. Organized time and organic time rarely keep time.

From an institutional perspective, this dissonance between organized and organic time is all too often reduced to a matter of 'time management' – how practitioners manage or fail to manage their time in accordance with the organized time of the institution. (Undergraduate students, doctoral students, lecturers and even professors are regularly informed that their problems could all be solved with better 'time management'!). From the perspective of the practitioner, this same dissonance is experienced as a matter not of 'time management', but of intellectual integrity – how to protect the organic time necessary to ensure the integrity of their own practice. The fact that this argument is sometimes misused by academics who rightly or wrongly see themselves as over-worked is not a good reason for entirely dismissing it. As Richard Sennett (1999) has argued, one of the prime consequences of the 'time management' regimes associated with late capitalist work places is 'the corrosion of character': the systematic effacement of continuity and growth and the denial of contingency and unpredictability (see also Sennett, 2008).

Pedagogy and Connectivity

Connectivity is *the* defining characteristic of the human agent. As Axel Honneth (1995, 125) reminds us, agency is always enacted within a force field of conflicting needs and interests: 'persons can feel themselves to be "valuable" only when they know themselves to be recognized for accomplishments that they precisely do not share in an undifferentiated manner with others'. My value to myself lies in your recognition of my difference; your value to yourself lies in my recognition of your difference. To be human is to crave difference *and* to desire the commonality necessary for our differences to be mutually recognized. Recognition necessarily involves mutuality. Not to have one's difference recognized is a form of disrespect, which (argues Honneth) expresses itself in acts of abuse and rape, exclusion and the denial of human rights and denigration and insult; the recognition of difference, on the other hand, is a precondition of 'basic self-confidence', 'self-respect' and 'self-esteem' (p. 129). To flourish is to have the capabilities and to enjoy the institutional conditions necessary for engaging in this 'struggle for recognition': a struggle for hospitality and the opening-up of boundaries.

Paul Ricoeur (2005), who acknowledges his considerable debt to the work of the much younger Honneth, sees recognition as a 'course', a process, the trajectory of which can be described in terms of its linguistic usage within philosophical discourse: 'my hypothesis is that potential philosophical uses of the verb *to recognize* can be organized along a trajectory running through its use in the active voice to its use in the passive voice' (p. 19). This 'reversal on the grammatical plane' he goes on to argue, shows 'the traces of a reversal of the same scope on the philosophical plane' (p. 19). Thus, to recognize in the active voice – 'to recognize as an act' – 'expresses a pretension, a claim, to exercise an intellectual mastery over this field of meanings, of signifying assertions'; while, at the opposite end of the trajectory, recognition in the passive voice – the demand to be recognized – 'expresses an expectation that can be satisfied only by mutual recognition, where this mutual recognition either remains an unfulfilled dream or requires procedures and institutions that elevate recognition to the political plane' (p. 19). The moral compass points towards recognition, mutuality and reciprocity as the defining features of pedagogic practice.

This 'course of recognition', as outlined by Ricouer, goes something like this: from a process of 'recognition as identification' – recognizing other things in the world; through a process of 'recognizing oneself' – identifying oneself in the world; to a process of 'mutual recognition' – being recognized as the object of other's identification. Ricoeur's grammatical analogy – from active to passive voice – is not intended to imply a movement from agency to lack of agency, but is attempting to locate the agent within a broader spectrum – or grammar – of mutuality and reciprocity; I become a person through an overlapping process which involves me in differentiating things in a world out there, identifying myself as an element within that differentiated world, and acknowledging that myriad others are involved in this process of mutual recognition. It is in part a life saga not only of the passage from cradle to grave, but also something of a psycho drama involving the historical layering of that saga in the here and now. To follow the grammatical analogy, the relation between the 'I' and the 'me' – the 'I' as identifying agent and the 'me' as identified subject – is mutually dependent; 'I' has no validity without a 'me', and 'me' has no substance without an 'I'. We each flourish – grow and distinguish ourselves – one with another.

Ricoeur's 'course' is, then, a kind of lifelong curriculum, a curriculum-in-the-making: a *curriculum vitae.* An underlying principle of this curriculum-not-yet-finished is that becoming and knowing cannot be unravelled into the tidy compartments of ontology and epistemology. Being, becoming and knowing are complicatedly entangled, knotted: what I am – and become – is what and how I know; what and how I know is what I am – and become. Ricoeur is suggesting that when and if we ever come to untangle the knot, the notion of mutual recognition may be a useful starting point – and, also, an end point: 'the course of self-recognition ends in mutual recognition' (p. 107). The recognition of self involves the recognition of others who in turn confer selfhood upon oneself as another: that, in part at least, is what Ricoeur means by human development through the mutuality and reciprocity of recognition. We grow up through an understanding of ourselves as differentiated, sentient beings within a world of other differentiated, sentient beings.

Recognition – as 'struggle' in the case of Honneth or as 'course' in the case of Ricoeur – necessarily involves, as a prime component, mutuality. It also involves, as a second necessary component, the acknowledgement of equal worth: 'the struggle for recognition', as Charles Taylor (1994, 50) puts it, 'can find only one satisfactory solution, and that is a regime of reciprocal recognition among equals'. Any such regime requires, as a third necessary component, impartiality of treatment in respect of difference, such 'that each person should enjoy the impartial treatment of their claims; that is, treatment based on principles that can be universally shared' (Held, 2010, 46). These three components – mutuality and reciprocity, the recognition of equal worth and impartiality of treatment – constitute the key elements of an ethics of connectivity as applied both to pedagogic practice and to the institutions whose prime purpose it is to sustain such practice.

Pedagogy, in other words, is hospitable. Derrida (2001, 16–17) identifies the ethical dimension of the civic with what he calls 'hospitality'. Indeed, he argues that the phrase 'ethic of hospitality' is 'tautologous'. So thoroughly coextensive is hospitality with the experience of hospitality that '*ethics is hospitality*' (original emphasis):

> Hospitality is culture itself and not simply one ethic amongst others. Insofar as it has to do with the *ethos*, that is, the residence, one's home, the familiar place of dwelling, inasmuch as it is a manner of being there, the manner in which we relate to ourselves and to others, to others as our own or as foreigners, *ethics is hospitality*; ethics is so thoroughly coextensive with the experience of hospitality.

Recalling Dante ('banished from Florence and then welcomed, it would seem, at Ravenna') Derrida traces the genealogy of 'hospitality' in relation to 'the city'. In the medieval tradition, one can identify what he calls 'a certain sovereignty of the city', so that 'the city itself could determine the laws of hospitality, the articles of predetermined law, both plural and restrictive, with which they meant to condition the Great Law of Hospitality – an unconditional law, both singular and universal, which ordered that the borders be open to each and every one, to every other, to all who might come, without question or without their even having to identify who they are or whence they came'.

The argument is, as always with Derrida, working hard on a lot of fronts: not least of which is the implied comparison between what he calls 'the Great Law of Hospitality' and much current legislation relating to the treatment and status of cross-border refugees (which is far from hospitable). He argues that the civic virtues necessarily inflect towards the hospitable. If the social sphere requires and is conditional upon an ethics of recognition, then the civic sphere is premised on an ethics of hospitality. To develop as a citizen is to learn how to be hospitable; how to be open and receptive to others; how to practice civic engagement as inclusion; how to see boundaries as permeable and negotiable. The civic is an open space in which we learn how to be open – and pedagogy is the means by which we acquire the capabilities necessary to take collective possession of that space.

***

The ethical impulse implicit in pedagogic practice is outward and expansive. Its characteristic gesture is that of reaching out both to what is as yet unknown and to new constituencies of learners. It transgresses disciplinary and institutional boundaries and (as the University of Central Asia illustrates) the cultural and geographical boundaries of nation states. The purpose of pedagogy – ethically and politically understood – is to develop and sustain an educated public capable of deliberating on matters of collective concern within an indeterminate world of cosmopolitan plurality and difference. The use of 'professional ethics' as a means of managing and controlling the academic workforce is wholly inimical to this larger ethical project. That project is oriented to the future and to the increasing globalization of time and space. We live in multiple time zones, the multiplicity of which influences how we understand our world and how our world is constituted through those understandings. Pedagogy invites us out into that world.

Chapter 10

Pedagogic Spaces

. . . which means 'dragon soaring in the sky'.

(Xiang Li, 2011, 51)

In the opening chapter, I argued for the university as one of the prime places of pedagogy – one of the places that exists with the purpose of not only supporting teaching and learning, but also reflecting on the significance of teaching and learning for human flourishing across generations. My starting point was the failure of universities – placed as they now are within an increasingly competitive marketplace – to orientate themselves towards these ends and purposes. One of the prime purposes of this book has been to highlight that failure and to point to new beginnings. Universities are one of the prime places within which we learn together how to become thoughtful, attentive, worldly and responsive. Insofar as they fulfil that purpose, they do so through pedagogic processes that rely on the meeting of minds – the 'fusion of horizons' – and on openness and dissensus: processes that reflect the scalar complexity of the world we inhabit. If the university is the institutional place of pedagogy, then relationality and interconnectivity comprise the more abstract and ubiquitous spaces of pedagogic practice: spaces of dissensus and difference, openness and opportunity.

Prologue: The Story of Xiang Li

In Feng Su's (2011) *Chinese Learning Journeys: Chasing the Dream*, Xiang Li recounts her experience as an undergraduate student at an English University (Li, 2011):

> My name is Xiang Li, and I was born in Shenzhen in the spring of 1988. Because my sign of the zodiac was the dragon, my parents named me *Xiang*, which means 'dragon soaring in the sky', in the hope that one

day their daughter would reach the summit of success . . . My parents numbered among the few fortunate university graduates to be assigned work after the period of Cultural Revolution. (Li, 2011, 51)

Xiang Li experienced what she calls 'a frustrating and bumpy road' in her school years and 'ended up in a top university in Guangzhou province instead of my first choice, which was the University of Hong Kong' (p. 53). English was her main subject. As a result of her faculty introducing 'a 2 + 2 collaboration programme with a tertiary institute in the north west of England which had recently obtained university status', she was able to go on exchange to the UK for her third and fourth years' study.

In 'rising to the challenges of studying in the UK', Xiang Li had to struggle with her own language development in English. This impacted both culturally and conceptually: 'I found myself hesitating over how to reply to questions such as "How are you?", "You all right?" or taking the initiative to greet people in this way' (pp. 56–57). She also experienced other varieties of English from fellow international students: 'Indian English, Korean English and African English' (p. 57). She became 'a very loyal fan of the BBC'. In the course of following BBC programmes with a view to improving her English, she began to see her own country of origin from different perspectives: 'I could see that my motherland China has been the target of criticism and its actions and policies with regard to human rights and Tibet, for instance, were often interpreted rather negatively' (p. 57).

Xiang Li was also 'coping with different learning styles'. She learnt to find her way around the library and 'realized that the tutor–student relationship can be so pivotal in students' study' (pp. 58–59). But she was also meeting people who she now realizes 'have shaped my views of the world'. This is the point at which Xiang Li's story gains huge pedagogical significance: in the persons of Mark, a business tutor, Margaret and Anne.

Mark confounded Xiang Li's view of black, sixty-two-year-old mature students. Mark was a 'gentleman' who was 'studying sociology and politics and was full of energy' – 'and even knew more about Chinese history than I did' (p. 63). Xiang Li's business studies tutor 'was aware of the Chinese student's limited understanding of slang, so she explained every slang expression she used in lectures . . . [W]e discussed many things, from essays and study, to personal issues such as how to get along with people and cope with a new culture' (p. 64). Margaret was a mature student: 'I developed a deep friendship with a note-taker, Margaret (who sat next to her blind client in order to read out notes during the lecture). Each time I came to the seminar, I brought some questions with me and discussed some political or culturally sensitive issues with her and enjoyed this' (pp. 64–65). Anne was 'a British-born Chinese classmate from my linguistic module whose family originated from Hong Kong' (p. 65): 'we communicated in both English and Cantonese, and Anne tended to switch to English in most cases' (pp. 65–66).

Xiang Li concludes the story of her 'learning journey' by telling her readers: 'During my stay in England, I not only improved my English proficiency but also broadened my horizons and world view as I attempted to do many things for the first time in my life'. Reading her story, we are aware of the complex relationality that accompanies and supports learning. Some of that relationality is contingent – a matter of luck; some of it is in part at least the result of design; most is a rather ragged mixture of both. Relationship mattered to Xiang Li. Those 'significant others' – a tutor and fellow students – that she met on her 'learning journey' were educationally important and pedagogically significant.

Pedagogy as a Practice

Pedagogy is, first and foremost, a practice. Insofar as it is a practice, it is social: it is what happens when practitioners act within a social context that recognizes and values their actions. Insofar as it is social, it is interconnective in its processes and cosmopolitan in its outreach. Those actions, collectively understood as having a collective purpose, constitute a practice. Pedagogy is, in part, the social glue whereby society coheres around particular norms. But because that cohesion relies crucially and increasingly on the recognition of different values – values that resist and even oppose cohesion – pedagogy also defines itself in critical relation to those norms. Pedagogy inflects two ways: towards consensus and towards dissensus. As consensus, it is centrally concerned with how dissensus is comprehended and integrated into a comprehensive and shared mode of understanding; as dissensus it is centrally concerned with resisting any such comprehensive and shared mode of understanding and with refusing foreclosure.

Located within a broader framework, this is the tension between equality and liberty: equality inflecting towards the homogenous; liberty inflecting towards the heterogeneous. But, of course, life is not quite as simple as that. We have to understand the social dimension of pedagogic practice as a kind of ongoing quarrel with that rather too easy dichotomy. Equality does not have to focus on sameness; liberty does not have to focus on the individuality of the individual: equality can take cognizance of difference and liberty can encompass collectivity. What the political theorist Chantal Mouffe (2005, 117) writes of democratic politics is true, also, of pedagogy conceived as a democratic practice: 'the crucial problem is how to transform *antagonism* into *agonism* . . . to provide the framework through which conflicts can take the form of an agonistic confrontation among adversaries instead of manifesting themselves as an antagonistic struggle between enemies' (original emphasis). How one addresses that problem, and whether or not one perceives it to be a problem, depends in large measure on the tradition within which the practice of pedagogy is framed.

All practices must reproduce themselves over time and, if they are to survive, across generations. This continuity is achieved through traditions of practice whereby the 'goods' intrinsic to that practice – dispositions, understandings, know-how – are passed on. These traditions become institutionalized over time, but their relation to the institutions with which they become associated may vary considerably; some institutions become central to the continuity of a particular tradition, while others may be peripheral and/or provisional. Chess could probably survive without its chess clubs, but the practice of medicine would be unsustainable without hospitals. Pedagogy as a practice is loosely attached to various institutional settings, but is tightly embedded within institutions specifically designated as institutions of education and of higher education.

In order to enable practices to reproduce themselves, traditions of practice and the institutional frameworks within which they operate must be responsive to changing circumstances and when necessary and appropriate adapt accordingly. This openness to change necessarily brings with it discontinuities and disjunctions without which traditions of practice close in on themselves and eventually close down. However, those same traditions of practice also require continuities and consistencies without which they would risk complete dispersal and eventual disintegration. This ongoing process of nurture and renewal is essential for the sustainability of any practice – whether it be farming, plumbing or indeed pedagogy. The historical dimension of practice necessarily extends towards openness and receptivity, on the one hand, and towards closure and containment on the other.

Pedagogic practice can be placed in relation to these two intersecting axes: the social axis (dissensus/consensus) and the temporal axis (open/closed). That simple configuration enables us to distinguish different orientations within and across the field of pedagogical practice (see Figure 1.)

		Social	
		Dissensus	Consensus
Temporal	Closed	I	II
	Open	IV	III

Figure 1 The dimensions of pedagogic practice

Of course, pedagogic practice does not fit neatly into any one of these cells. However, the schema does provide some insights into the underlying codes of pedagogic practice. For example, practices located in Cell I are open to disagreement but closed to change, while those located in Cell II prioritize both assent and stasis. Cell I questions might be nominally open, but would assume a strictly limited range of responses; Cell II questions would be closed and would assume a 'right' answer. In both Cells I and II, there are strict limits to what it is legitimate to render problematic, although in the case of Cell I there is greater latitude regarding what it is legitimate to discuss. If a value premium is placed on the openness and unpredictability of learning, then neither Cell 1 nor Cell II practices fare particularly well; if a value is placed on dissensus and the exploration of divergent and opposing viewpoints, then Cell I fares better than Cell II.

One could imagine practitioners operating in Cell I employing discursive modes of pedagogy, but within a formalized system that determined the outcomes of the discussion. Similarly, one could imagine that practitioners operating in Cell II would be more likely to routinely adopt a more didactic style of teaching. Both would place a strong emphasis on conformity as a measure of institutional excellence and of discipline as an indicator of individual worth. Cells I and II might well be seen as peripheral to mainstream pedagogic practice as conceived by practitioners themselves, although many of the systems of higher education and the expectations laid on those institutions by managers, policy makers and politicians would suggest that the practices associated with what I am terming 'closure' are far from merely residual. They continue to exert a strong influence on the experience of teaching and learning in universities and on how higher education is perceived and valued.

Cell III has a stronger presence within the higher education sector and might well be seen as the dominant mode. Here the emphasis is on consensus regarding targets, outcomes and criteria, but within a context which privileges change and innovation. Key phrases in the lexicon of Cell III include, for example, 'problem-solving' (where the problem is given), 'team-building' (where the team constitutes a group-in-agreement) and 'active learning' (where the activities are prescribed and their outcomes determined). Cell III practitioners are likely to see themselves as 'progressive'. There is likely to be an emphasis on learning how to learn, with the possible assumption that there are certain generic procedures or methods that can be abstracted from their specific contexts and then applied across a range of contexts. Such an assumption sits easily with dominant models of vocational education, professional education and research training. Cell III, in other words, easily accommodates programmes of study at undergraduate, postgraduate taught and postgraduate research levels.

Pedagogic practice within Cell III undoubtedly addresses some interesting pedagogical problems: for example, how to engage and motivate students, how to ensure 'relevance', how to broaden higher education and beyond an exclusive concern with the transmission of received information. However, as Louis Menand (2010, 19) points out, these are no longer problems which 'test the limits of the system'. They now sit fairly easily within those limits: 'once, being a professor meant (among other things) possessing, by dint of years immersed in library mineshafts, refinements on knowledge that were effectively inaccessible to the unlearned person. Now, most of that esoterica is available instantly on Wikipedia. Sheer information is no longer a major piece of the value-added of higher education'. Acknowledging the unprecedented availability and accessibility of knowledge is now part of received pedagogical wisdom: part of what 'being a professor' necessarily entails.

Dissensus and Relationality

The problems that continue not only to 'test the limits of the system' but also to challenge that system are those associated with Cell IV. Here pedagogy struggles with the problem of how in a complex and interconnected world to acknowledge the conflicting demands of both dissensus (in respect of commitment to value) and consensus (in respect of commitment to action). This is what Chantal Mouffe (2005) terms 'the democratic paradox'. In her *The Return of the Political* (1993), she explains this paradox in the following terms:

> A pluralist democracy is constantly pulled in opposite directions: towards exacerbation of differences and disintegration on one side; towards homogenization and strong forms of unity on the other. I consider . . . that

> the specificity of modern democracy as a new political form of society, as a new 'regime', lays precisely in the *tension* between the democratic logic of equality and the liberal logic of liberty. It is a tension that we should value and protect, rather than try to resolve, because it is constitutive of pluralist democracy. (p. 150) (original emphasis)

Mouffe argues that what is required is civic engagement and that what, in turn, civic engagement requires is value pluralism: 'we need to make room for the pluralism of cultures, collective forms of life and regimes, as well as the pluralism of subjects, individual choices and the conceptions of the good' (p. 151). This has important consequences not only for politics but also for education. Value pluralism, she maintains, can only be sustained 'by developing and multiplying in as many social relations as possible, the discourses, the practices, the "language games" that produce democratic "subject positions". The objective is to establish the hegemony of democratic values and practices' (p. 151). The fulfilment of that objective presupposes dissensus in respect of social discourse and openness in respect of the future.

The question that then arises is how dissensus can be sustained within an agreed pedagogic framework: how to ensure that the framework does not simply buckle under the strain of dissensus. What agreements constitute the conditions necessary for the exploration of disagreement within a pluralist and cosmopolitan society? How might we proceed with – as Arendt puts it – 'no pillars and props'? What are the relational conditions necessary for the development of human understanding?

First, within any pedagogic relationship, there must be a shared understanding that understanding itself matters and that what one is seeking to understand is a worthwhile object of enquiry. In order for the pedagogical relationship to work, both teacher and taught must agree that understanding matters and that it matters in the context of this particular enquiry. Within our tabloid and celebrity culture, understanding is in short supply. Regarding certain sorts of criminal behaviours, for example, the immediate response is one of condemnation and recrimination. Indeed, to seek to understand certain sorts of behaviour is considered inappropriate or plain wrong. Under such circumstances, to seek to understand is confused with 'making excuses for' or 'justifying' that which is deemed inexcusable or beyond justification. Understanding is rendered out of bounds.

Second, there must be agreement that disagreement is worthwhile and that the acknowledgement of divergent and sometimes diametrically opposed views is an essential element in the process of understanding.

Divergent or opposing viewpoints are often difficult to receive and engage with – which is precisely why they are 'divergent' or 'opposing'. We have to approach understanding with a recognition that difficulty is integral to the process. To seek to understand is in part at least to discover what is difficult in that which one is seeking to understand. Difficulty is the stuff of understanding. This again cuts across the grain of a sound bite culture that prizes instant gratification and immediacy of communication.

Third, the pedagogic relationship must agree on the long-term open-endedness of all human understanding. These are necessary conditions of all human understanding – the non-negotiables without which any attempt at understanding will prove baseless. This takes us back to the question-and-answer cycle that (as we saw in Chapters 3 and 8, respectively) Gadamer highlights and Collingwood exemplifies: answers generate questions, which prompt further responses, which in turn generate new questions, etc. Resolutions are provisional; settlements are conditional; insights are cumulative. Understanding is premised on uncertainty and indeterminacy. Unless those involved in the pedagogic relationship can dwell with that uncertainty and indeterminacy, understanding is unworkable.

Pedagogy is centrally concerned with these underlying agreements without which understanding is impossible. We cannot seek to understand unless we acknowledge that understanding is worthwhile and that what we are seeking to understand is at least potentially worth understanding. We cannot reason together unless we listen to one another. We cannot understand if we demand easy and immediate answers. These are the preconditions of understanding. Crucially, however, they cannot usefully be reduced to a set of rules. They require a personal commitment and the dispositions that follow from that commitment. Within the space of the pedagogic relationship, they require a willingness to trust.

Relationality and Openness

Trust is an easy notion to evoke, but a difficult one to apply unless the conditions for trust already exist. In his 'ten dispatches about place', Berger (2007, 114) writes about the situation of the displaced: 'they are beside the place they chose to come to. The distance which separates them from it is incalculable. Maybe it's only the width of a thoroughfare, maybe it's a world away. The place has lost what made it a destination. It has lost its territory of experience'. This experience of displacement – of the loss of the 'territory of experience' – has always been a defining feature of the human condition for much of the world's population. Jamil Ahmed (2011), Mourid Barghouti (2004), Mahmoud Darwish (2007), to name but a few, have expressed in story, autobiography and poetry what that loss means for particular groups in particular places within the current context of geopolitical upheaval.

We require pedagogies that speak to the particularity of these conditions. That is why Appiah's (2005, 213) notion of 'a tenable cosmopolitanism' – or 'rooted cosmopolitanism' – has such purchase: 'a cosmopolitanism with prospects must reconcile a kind of universalism with the legitimacy of at least some forms of partiality' (p. 223) (see also Appiah, 2006). A cosmopolitan outlook does not necessitate or even encourage an uprooting of affiliation and association from the partial to the universal, although it does necessarily involve shifts of perspective. 'Rooted cosmopolitanism' may be grounded in the particularities of local loyalty and community while branching out into the civic and flourishing within the broader interconnectivities of the global. There is a need for higher education practices that develop the cosmopolitan dispositions necessary for this rooting and flourishing: this recognition of the interdependency of the local and the global; this sense of the global-in-the-local and the local-in-the-global.

Traditionally, the public good has been defined in terms of what was good for the locality and the nation. The idea of community education encapsulates this sense of education as being a common good to be shared as an entitlement by all members of the community. Within the higher education sector of the UK, the older 'civic' universities and the post-Robbins, post-1992 and more recent universities continue to draw a significant proportion of their undergraduate student population from within the broad region. They very often developed from earlier institutions that were rooted in local trades and industries with which they may retain historic partnerships that are reflected in their particular specialism and areas of academic excellence. Similarly, the community colleges and state universities within the US system reflect and respond to the particular needs and priorities of the locality and state.

An ethic of 'rooted cosmopolitanism' values these institutional loyalties and affiliations, but locates them within a broader cosmopolitan vision. The rooted particularity of the institution and its history and of the students and their backgrounds is of supreme importance. However, that rooted particularity is now being shaped by a process of '*really existing cosmopolitanization*', the impact and significance of which can only be understood by really existing people who seek to relate its impact and significance to their own and others' really existing circumstances. Conceived in this way, cosmopolitanism is not some kind of ethical abstract, but involves recognition of our global interconnectivities and interdependencies and an acknowledgement of the need for collective responses to challenges that, although global, are experienced as local and contingent. They are experienced, that is, differentially. 'Rooted cosmopolitanism' reminds us of the deep inequalities implicit in these locally determined, global differentials.

It reminds us, also, of what Said (2004b, 80) termed 'widening circles of pertinence'. He warned against 'the leap to mobilized collective selves – without careful transition or deliberate reflection or with only unmediated assertion – that prove to be more destructive than anything they are supposedly defending'. These 'transitionless leaps' lead to 'totalities, unknowable existentially but powerfully mobilizing'; they are forceful 'exactly because they are corporate and can stand in unjustifiably for action that is supposed to be careful, measured and humane'. A 'rooted cosmopolitanism', refusing these leaps into totalizing universals, widens its 'circles of pertinence' carefully, with measured pace, and humanely.

The word 'humane' should be a privileged item in the lexicon of 'rooted cosmopolitanism', for as Said goes on to argue 'the only word to break up the leap to such corporate banditry is the word "humane", and humanists without an exfoliating, elaborating, demystifying general humaneness are, as the phrase has it, sounding brass and tinkling cymbals' (p. 81). To be 'humane' is to abandon, as 'the abiding basis for all humanistic practice', any premature recourse to 'general or even concrete statements about vast structures of power' or to 'vaguely therapeutic structures of salutary redemption': it is to be concerned with, and attentive to, 'human beings who exist in history' (p. 61). The worldliness ('secularity') implicit in cosmopolitanism does not and should not imply any lack of *locus*, of place. On the contrary, to be worldly is to be situated – as a human being who exists in history – within the world.

***

As David Harvey (2010, 231) points out: 'this is utopian! But so what! We cannot afford not to be'. We cannot, that is, afford a higher education system that is unequal in its allocation of resources and talent and that manifestly fails – at the point of entry and exit – the mass of students from lower socio-economic backgrounds. This system is not only unfair, but also potentially disastrous in its economic and social consequences. For the sake of the future, those with power and influence must acknowledge and respond to the need for a genuinely egalitarian system of public higher education that allows for social mobility, genuine equality of opportunity at every level of the system, and maximum flexibility and creativity. That will be costly, but we must decide whether we want to perpetuate a deeply unequal system of higher education or whether we want a public higher education system that offers the possibility of new beginnings regardless of origins. That is the challenge. We in the privileged West might well look to other regions of the world for the necessary resources of hope to meet this challenge – and, indeed, to face down the constant riposte that utopias are unrealizable.

References

Achebe, C. (2010) *An Image of Africa.* London: Penguin Books.

Ahmed, J. (2011) *The Wandering Falcon.* London: Hamish Hamilton.

Agamben, G. (2007) *Infancy and History: The Destruction of Experience* (Trans. L. Heron). London and New York: Verso.

Appiah, K.A. (2005) *The Ethics of Identity.* Princeton: Princeton University Press.

— (2006) *Cosmopolitanism: Ethics in a World of Strangers.* New York: W.W. Norton.

Arendt, H. (1970a) *Men in Dark Times.* London: Jonathan Cape.

— (1970b) *On Violence.* Orlando, Austin, New York, San Diego and London: Harcourt, Inc.

— (1972) *Crises of the Republic.* New York: Harcourt Brace Jovanovich.

— (1973) *The Origins of Totalitarianism: New Edition with Added Prefaces.* San Diego, New York and London: Harcourt Brace and Company.

— (1978) *The Life of the Mind* (one-volume edition). San Diego, New York and London: Harcourt, Inc.

— (1993) *Between Past and Present: Eight Exercises in Political Thought,* Harmondsworth: Penguin Books.

— (1996) *Love and St Augustine* (edited by J.V. Scott and J.C. Stark). Chicago and London: The University of Chicago Press.

— (1998) *The Human Condition* (2nd Edition). Chicago and London: The University of Chicago Press.

— (2003) *Responsibility and Judgement* (ed. J. Kohn). New York: Schocken Books.

— (2006) *Eichmann in Jerusalem: A Report on the Banality of Evil.* London: Penguin Books.

Aristotle (1976) *The Ethics of Aristotle: The Nicomachean Ethics* (Trans. J.A.K. Thompson). London: Penguin Books.

Auerbach, E. (2003) *Mimesis: The Representation of Reality in Western Literature* (Trans. W.R. Trask). Princeton and Oxford: Princeton University Press. (1st published in 1953).

Baramki, G. (2010) *Peaceful Resistance: Building a Palestinian University Under Occupation.* London and New York: Pluto Press.

Barenboim, D. (2004) Sound and vision. *The Guardian Review,* (25 October) p. 15.

Barenboim, D. and Said, E.W. (2004) *Parallels and Paradoxes: Explorations in Music and Society* (edited and with a preface by A. Guzelimian). London: Bloomsbury.

Barghouti, M. (2004) *I Saw Ramallah* (Trans. A. Soueif). London: Bloomsbury.

Bauman, Z. (1987) *Legislators and Interpreters: On Modernity, Post-modernity and Intellectuals.* Cambridge: Polity Press.

Beck, U. (2009) *World at Risk.* Cambridge and Malden, MA: Polity.

Benhabib, S. (2000) Arendt's 'Eichmann in Jerusalem', in D. Villa (ed) *The Cambridge Companion to Hannah Arendt*. Cambridge, New York, Melbourne and Madrid: Cambridge University Press, pp. 65–85.
— (2010) International law and human plurality in the shadow of totalitarianism: Hannah Arendt and Raphael Lemkin, in S. Benhabib (ed) *Politics in Dark Times: Encounters with Hannah Arendt*. Cambridge: Cambridge University Press, pp. 219–243.
Berger, J. (1958) *A Painter of Our Time*. London: secker and Warburg.
— (1962) *The Foot of Clive*. London: Methuen.
— (1964) *Corker's Freedom*. London: Methuen.
— (1969a) *Art and Revolution: Ernst Neizvestny and the Role of the Artist in the USSR*. Harmondsworth: Penguin Books.
— (1969b) *The Moment of Cubism and Other Essays*. London: Weidenfeld and Nicolson.
— (1972a) *Selected Essays and Articles: the Look of Things*. Harmondsworth: Penguin.
— (1972b) *Ways of Seeing*. Harmondsworth: Penguin.
— (1974) Introduction: a philosopher and death, in E. Fischer *An Opposing Man* (Trans P. and B. Ross). London: Allen Lane.
— (1979) *Permanent Red: Essays in Seeing*. London and New York: Writers and Readers Publishing Cooperative. (1st published 1960).
— (1980) *About Looking*. London: Writers and Readers.
— (1984) *And Our Faces, My Heart, Brief as Photos*. London: Writers and Readers.
— (1985) *G*. London: Chatto and Windus The Hogarth Press. (1st published 1972).
— (1992) *Into Their Labours: Pig Earth, Once in Europa, Lilac and Flag*. London: Granta Books in association with Penguin Books.
— (1995) *To the Wedding*. London: Bloomsbury.
— (1996) *Photocopies*. London: Bloomsbury.
— (2001) *The Shape of a Pocket*. London: Bloomsbury.
— (2005) *Here Is Where We Meet*. London: Bloomsbury.
— (2007a) *Hold Everything Dear: Dispatches on Survival and Resistance*. London and New York: Verso.
— (2007b) *Berger on Drawing* (2nd Edition). Aghabullogue, Co. Cork: Occasional Press.
— (2008) *From A to X. A Story in Letters*. London and New York: Verso.
— (2011) *Bento's Sketchbook*. London and New York: Verso.
Berger, J. and Mohr, J. (1967) *A Fortunate Man*. Harmondsworth: Penguin Books.
— (1975) *A Seventh Man: A Book of Images and Words about the Experience of Migrant Workers in Europe*. Harmondsworth: Penguin Books.
Berlin, I. (1996) The sense of reality, in I. Berlin (ed) *The Sense of Reality: Studies in Ideas and their History* (ed. H. Hardy). London: Pimlico/Random House, pp. 1–39.
Bernstein, R.J. (2000) Arendt on thinking, in D. Villa (ed) *The Cambridge Companion to Hannah Arendt*. Cambridge, New York, Melbourne and Madrid: Cambridge University Press, pp. 277–292.
Bhaba, H. (2005) Adagio, in H. Bhaba and W.J.T. Mitchell (eds) *Edward Said: Continuing the Conversation*. Chicago and London: The University of Chicago Press, pp. 7–16.

Bilsky, L. (2010) The Eichmann trial and the legacy of jurisdiction, in S. Benhabib (ed) *Politics in Dark Times: Encounters with Hannah Arendt*. Cambridge: Cambridge University Press, pp. 198–218.

Bingham, T. (2010) *The Rule of Law*. London: Allen Lane.

Bird, M. (2008) *The St Ives Artists: A Biography of Place and Time*. Aldershot and Burlington: Lund Humphries.

Bok, D. (2003) *Universities in the Marketplace: the Commercialization of Higher Education*. Princeton, NJ: Princeton University Press.

Bowlby, J. (1973) *Attachment and Loss*. Vol. 2: *Separation: Anxiety and Anger*. New York: Basic Books.

— (1980) *Attachment and Loss*. Vol. 3: *Loss: Sadness and Depression*. New York: Basic Books.

— (1982) *Attachment and Loss*. Vol. 1: *Attachment* (2nd Edition). New York: Basic Books.

Brightman, C. (ed) (1995) *Between Friends: The Correspondence of Hannah Arendt and Mary McCarthy 1949–1975*. London: Secker and Warburg.

Brown, R. (ed) (2011) *Higher Education and the Market*. London and New York: Routledge.

Collingwood, R.G. (1978) *An Autobiography*. Oxford: Oxford University Press. (1st published 1939).

Collini, S. (2006) *Absent Minds: Intellectuals in Britain*. Oxford and New York: Oxford University Press.

— (2011) From Robbins to McKinsey. *London Review of Books*, 33, 16, 9–14.

Curtius, E.R. (1990) *European Literature and the Latin Middle Ages*. Bollingen Series XXXVI. (Trans. W.R. Trask). Princeton, NJ: Princeton University Press. (1st published in 1953).

Darwish, M. (2007) *The Butterfly's Burden* (Trans. F. Joudah). Tarset, Northumberland: Bloodaxe.

Department for Business, Innovation and Skills (2011) *Higher Education: Students at the Heart of the System*. London: Department for Business, Innovation and Skills.

Derrida, J. (2001) *On Cosmopolitanism and Forgiveness* (Trans. M. Dooley and M. Hughes). London and New York: Routledge/Taylor and Francis Group.

Duarte, E. (2001) The eclipse of thinking: an Arendtian critique of cooperative learning, in M. Gordon (ed) *Hannah Arendt and Education: Renewing Our Common World*. Boulder, Col and Oxford: Westview Press, pp. 201–223.

Dunne, J. (1997) *Back to the Rough Ground: Practical Judgment and the Lure of Technique*. Notre Dame, Indiana: University of Notre Dame Press.

Dworkin, R. (2011a) *Justice for Hedgehogs*. Cambridge, Mass., and London: The Belknap Press of Harvard University Press.

— (2011b) What is a good life? *The New York Review*. LVIII, 2, 41–43.

Dyer, G. (1986) *Ways of Telling: The Work of John Berger*. London: Pluto Press.

Ecclestone, K. and Hayes, D. (2009) *The Dangerous Rise of Therapeutic Education*. London: Routledge.

Economic and Social Research Council (ESRC) (2008) *Widening Participation in Higher Education: A Commentary by the Teaching and Learning Research Programme*. London: Teaching and Learning Research Programme, ESRC.

Elliott, L. (2011) We've been warned: the system is ready to blow. *The Guardian*, (15 August) p. 23.

Elon, A. (2006) The excommunication of Hannah Arendt, in H. Arendt *Eichmann in Jerusalem: A Report on the Banality of Evil*. London: Penguin Books, pp. vii–xxiii.

Ettinger, E. (1995) *Hannah Arendt Martin Heidegger*. New Haven and London: Yale University Press.

Fischer, E. (1969) *Art Against Ideology*. Harmondsworth: Penguin.

— (1974) *An Opposing Man* (Trans P. and B. Ross). London: Allen Llane.

— (2010) *The Necessity of Art* (Trans. A. Bostock). London and New York: Verso. (1st published in English 1963).

Gadamer, H.-G. (1977) *Philosophical Hermeneutics* (ed. and Trans. D.E. Ling). Berkely, Los Angeles and London: University of California Press.

— (2001) *Gadamer in Conversation: Reflections and Commentary* (ed. and Trans. R.E. Palmer). New Haven and London: Yale University Press.

— (2004) *Truth and Method* (Trans. J. Weinsheimer and D.G. Marshall) (2nd Revised Edition). London and New York: Continuum.

— (2006) *A Century of Philosophy: Hans-Georg Gadamer in Conversation with Riccardo Dottori* (Trans. R. Coltman with S. Koepke). New York and London: Continuum.

Harvey, D. (2010) *The Enigma of Capital and the Crises of Capitalism*. London: Profile Books.

Hattersley, R. (2004) Education and the good society (1), in F. Inglis (ed) *Education and the Good Society*. Basingstoke, UK and New York: Palgrave Macmillan, pp. 12–22.

Head, S. (2011) The grim threat to British universities. *The New York Review*, LVIII, 1, 58–64.

Heidegger, M. (1962) *Being and Time* (Trans. J. Macquarrie and E. Robinson). New York: Harper and Row.

Held, D. (2010) *Cosmopolitanism: Ideals and Realities*. Cambridge and Malden, MA: Polity.

Heller, D.E. (2007) Financing public research universities in the United States: the role of students and their families, in R.L. Geiger, C.L. Colbeck, R.L. Williams and C.K. Anderson (eds) *Future of the American Public Research University*. Rotterdam and Taipei: Sense Publishers.

Hill, M.A. (1979) *Hannah Arendt: The Recovery of the Public World*. New York: St Martin's Press.

Hind, D. (2010) *The Return of the Public*. London and New York: Verso.

Hobsbawm, E. (1995) *Age of Extremes: The Short Twentieth Century 1914–1991*. London: Abacus.

Hoggart, R. (1957) *The Uses of Literacy: Aspects of Working-class Life, with Special References to Publications and Entertainments*. London: Chatto and Windus.

Honneth, A. (1995) *The Struggle for Recognition: the Moral Grammar of Social Conflicts* (Trans. J. Anderson). Cambridge: Polity Press.

Hotson, H. (2011) Don't look to the Ivy League. *London Review of Books*, 33, 10, 20–22.

Hutton, W. (2010) The financial crisis and the need of the hunter-gatherer, in R. Williams and L. Elliott (eds) *Crisis and Recovery: Ethics, Economics and Justice*. Houndmills and New York: Palgrave Macmillan, pp. 182–189.

Inglis, F. (2009) *History Man: The Life of R.G. Collingwood.* Princeton and Woodstock: Princeton University Press.

Jackson, B. and Segal, P. (2007) Equality, in A.H. Halsey with R. Hattersley and others, *Democracy in Crisis: Ethical Socialism for a Prosperous Country.* London: Politico's, pp. 102–134.

Jaspers, K. (1986) *Basic Philosophical Writings* (ed. E. Erlich, L.H. Erlich and G.B. Pepper). Athens: Ohio University Press.

Josipovici, G. (1999) *On Trust: Art and the Temptations of Suspicion.* New Haven and London: Yale University Press.

Judt, T. (2009) *Reappraisals: Reflections on the Forgotten Twentieth Century.* London: Vintage.

— (2010) *Postwar: A History of Europe Since 1945.* London: Vintage.

Kaletsky, A. (2010) *Capitalism 0.4: the Birth of New Economy.* London: Bloomsbury.

Kierkegaard, S. (1954) *Fear and Trembling and The Sickness Unto Death* (Trans. W. Lowrie). New York: Doubleday Anchor Books/Princeton University Press.

Kohler, L. (ed) (1996) *Within Four Walls: The Correspondence between Hannah Arendt and Heinrich Blucher 1936–1968* (Trans. P. Constantine). New York, San Diego and London: Harcourt, Inc.

Kristeva, J. (2001) *Hannah Arendt* (Trans. R. Guberman). New York: Columbia University Press.

Kuromiya, H. (2005) *Stalin.* Harlow: Pearson Longman.

Langer, S. (1967) *Mind: An Essay on Human Feeling Volume I.* Baltimore and London: The John Hopkins Press.

— (1972) *Mind: An Essay on Human Feeling Volume II.* Baltimore and London: The John Hopkins University Press.

— (1982) *Mind: An Essay on Human Feeling Volume III.* Baltimore and London: The John Hopkins University Press.

Lazerson, M. (2010) *Higher Education and the American Dream: Success and its Discontents.* Budapest and New York: Central University Press.

Leavis, F.R. (1932) *New Bearings in English Poetry: A Study of the Contemporary Situation.* London: Chatto and Windus.

— (1952) *The Common Pursuit.* London: Chatto and Windus.

— (1962) *Two Cultures? The Significance of C.P. Snow.* London: Chatto and Windus.

Li, X. (2011) An undergraduate student in Liverpool: a woman's struggle, in F. Su (ed) *Chinese Learning Journeys: Chasing the Dream.* Stoke on Trent, UK and Sterling, USA: Trentham Books.

Lieven, A. (2011) *Pakistan: A Hard Country.* New York: Public Affairs. (Published in Great Britain by Allen Lane).

MacIntyre, A. (1985) *After Virtue: A Study in Moral Theory* (2nd Edition). London: Duckworth.

Madrick, J. (2010) *The Case for Big Government.* Princeton and Oxford: Princeton University Press.

Maier-Katkin, D. (2010) *Stranger from Abroad: Hannah Arendt, Martin Heidegger, Friendship and Forgiveness.* London and New York: W.W. Norton and Company.

McKibbin, R. (2010) Good for business. *London Review of Books*, 32, 4, 9–10.

Menand, L. (2010) *The Marketplace of Ideas: Reform and Resistance in the American University.* New York and London: W.W. Norton and Co.

Mouffe, C. (1993) *The Return of the Political.* London and New York: Verso.

—(2005) *The Democratic Paradox.* London and New York: Verso.

Moyo, D. (2011) *How the West Was Lost: Fifty Years of Economic Folly – And the Stark Choices Ahead.* London: Allen Lane.

Neiman, S. (2002) *Evil in Modern Thought: An Alternative History of Philosophy.* Princeton and Woodstock: Princeton University Press.

—(2010) Banality reconsidered, in S. Benhabib (ed) *Politics in Dark Times: Encounters with Hannah Arendt.* Cambridge: Cambridge University Press, pp. 305–315.

Nixon, J. (2008) *Towards the Virtuous University: the Moral Bases of Academic Practice.* London and New York: Routledge.

—(2011a) *Higher Education and the Public Good: Imagining the University.* London and New York: Continuum.

—(2011b) Re-imagining the public good, in M. Bailey and D. Freedman (eds) *The Assault on Universities: A Manifesto for Resistance.* London: Pluto Press.

—(2011c) Universities and the common good, in R. Barnett (ed) *The Future University: Ideas and Possibilities.* London and New York: Routledge.

Nussbaum, M.C. (1990) *Love's Knowledge: Essays on Philosophy and Literature.* Oxford: Oxford University Press.

—(1994) *The Therapy of Desire: Theory and Practice in Hellenistic Ethics.* Princeton: Princeton University Press.

—(1995) *Poetic Justice: The Literary Imagination and Public Life.* (The Alexander Rosenthall Lectures Northwestern University Law School). Boston, Mass.: Beacon Press.

—(1997) *Cultivating Humanity: A Classical Defence of Reform in Liberal Education.* Cambridge, Mass., and London: Harvard University Press.

—(2000) *Women and Human Development: The Capabilities Approach.* Cambridge: Cambridge University Press.

—(2001a) *The Fragility of Goodness: Luck and Ethics in Greek Tragedy and Philosophy* Revised ed. Cambridge: Cambridge University Press.

—(2001b) *Upheavals of Thought: The Intelligence of Emotions.* Cambridge: Cambridge University Press.

—(2006) *Frontiers of Justice: Disability, Nationality, Species Membership.* Cambridge, MA: Harvard University Press.

—(2008) *Liberty of Conscience: In defence of America's Tradition of Religious Equality.* New York: Basic Books.

—(2010) *Not for Profit: Why Democracy Needs the Humanities.* Princeton and Oxford: Princeton University Press.

—(2011) *Creating Capabilities: The Human Development Approach.* Cambridge, Mass., and London: The Belknap Press of Harvard University Press.

Nussbaum, M.C. and Sen, A. (eds) (1993) *The Quality of Life.* A study prepared for the World Institute for Development Economic Research (WIDER) of the United Nations University. Oxford: Clarendon Press.

Oleksiyenko, A. (2012) 'Glonacal' partnership strategies in central Asia: private initiatives and public purpses in higher education, in B. Adamson, J. Nixon and F. Su (eds) *The Reorientation of Higher Education: Beyond the East-West Dichotomy.* Hong Kong: Comparative Education Research Centre (CERC) University of Hong Kong/Springer (Forthcoming).

O'Toole, F. (2009) *Ship of Fools: How Stupidity and Corruption Sank the Celtic Tiger.* London: Faber and Faber.

Paulin, T. (2004) Writing to the moment. *The Guardian Review,* (25 September) pp. 4–6.

Polanyi, M. (1958) *Personal Knowledge: Towards a Post-Critical Philosophy.* London: Routledge and Kegan Paul.

Polanyi, M. and Prosch, H. (1975) *Meaning.* Chicago: University of Chicago Press.

Raz, J. (2009) *Between Authority and Interpretation: On the Theory of Law and Practical Reason.* Oxford: Oxford University Press.

Read, H. (1951) *Contemporary British Art.* Harmondsworth: Penguin Books.

Reay, D., David, M. and Ball, S. (eds) (2005) *Degrees of Choice: Social Class, Race and Gender in Higher Education.* London: Trentham Books.

Ricoeur, P. (2005) *The Course of Recognition* (Trans. D. Pellaur). Cambridge, Mass., and London, England: Harvard University Press.

Ritzen, J. (2010) *A Chance for European Universities. Or: Avoiding the Looming University Crisis in Europe.* Amsterdam: Amsterdam University Press.

Said, E.W. (1993a) *Culture and Imperialism.* London: Chatto and Windus.

— (1993b) *After the Sky: Palestinian Lives* (Photographs by Jean Mohr). London Vintage. (1st published by Faber and Faber 1986).

— (1994) *Representations of Reality: the 1993 Reith Lectures.* London: Vintage/Random House.

— (1997a) *Covering Islam: How the Media and the Experts Determine How We See the Rest of the World.* London: Vintage Books. (1st published in 1981).

— (1997b) *Beginnings: Intention and Method.* London: Granta Books. (1st published in 1975).

— (1999) *Out of Place: A Memoir.* London: Granta Books.

— (2000) *Reflections on Exile and Other Essays.* Cambridge, Mass.: Harvard University Press.

— (2003a) *Orientalism.* London: Penguin. (1st published in 1978).

— (2003b) *Freud and the Non-European.* London and New York: Verso in association with the Freud Museum, London.

— (2004a) *Power, Politics and Culture: Interviews with Edward W. Said* (ed. G. Viswanathan). London: Bloomsbury.

— (2004b) *Humanism and Democratic Criticism.* New York: Columbia University Press.

— (2004c) *From Oslo to Iraq and the Roadmap* (Foreword by T. Judt and Afterword by W.E. Said). London: Bloomsbury Publishing Plc.

— (2006) *On Late Style.* London: Bloomsbury.

— (2009) *Music at the Limits: Three Decades of Essays and Articles on Music.* London, Berlin and New York: Bloomsbury.

— (2010) *The Pen and the Sword: Conversations with Edward Said.* Chicago, Illinois: Haymarket Books.

Schlingensiepen, F. (2010) *Deitrich Bonhoeffer 1906–1945: Martyr, Thinker, Man of Resistance* (Trans I Best). London and New York: Continuum.

Sen, A. (1999) *Development as Freedom.* Oxford: Oxford University Press.

Sennett, R. (1999) *The Corrosion of Character: The Personal Consequences of Work in the New Capitalism.* New York and London: W.W. Norton and Company.

—(2008) *The Craftsman*. London: Allen Lane/Penguin Books.

Shumar, W. (1997) *College for Sale*. London and Washington DC: Falmer Press.

Skinner, Q. (2003a) *Visions of Politics. Volume 1: Regarding Method*. Cambridge: Cambridge University Press.

—(2003b) *Volume 2: Renaissance Virtues*. Cambridge: Cambridge University Press.

—(2003c) *Volume 3: Hobbes and Civil Society*. Cambridge: Cambridge University Press.

Smith, H. (2008) Spoon-feeding: or how I learned to stop worrying and love the mess. *Teaching in Higher Education*, 13, 6, 715–718.

Snow, C.P. (1993) *The Two Cultures* (with an introduction by Stefan Collini). Cambridge: Cambridge University Press.

Snyder, T. (2010) *Bloodlands: Europe Between Hitler and Stalin*. London: The Bodley Head.

Soros, G. (2010) *The Soros Lectures at the Central European University*. New York: Public Affairs.

Standish, P. (2012) Teaching in the university the day after tomorrow, in R. Barnett (ed) *The Future University: Ideas and Possibilities*. New York and Abingdon: Routledge.

Stiglitz, J.E. (2010) *Freefall: Free Markets and the Sinking of the Global Economy*. London: Allen Lane/Penguin Books.

Su, F. (ed) (2011) *Chinese Learning Journeys: Chasing the Dream*. Stoke on Trent, UK and Sterling, USA: Trentham Books.

Sutton Trust (2004) *The Missing 3000: State School Students Under-represented at Leading Universities*. London: The Sutton Trust (August).

—(2008) *University Admissions by Individual Schools*. London: The Sutton Trust (February).

Szirtes, G. (2011) A horse, a circus and a small case of photographs, in P. Baki, C. Ford and G. Szirtes (eds) *Eyewitness. Hungarian Photography in the Twentieth Century: Brassai, Capa, Kertesz, Maholy-Nagy, Munkacsi*. London: Royal Academy of Arts.

Taylor, C. (1994) The politics of recognition, in A. Gutman (ed) *Multiculturalism: Examining the Politics of Recognition* (2nd Edition). Princeton: Princeton University Press, pp. 25–73. (Lecture inaugurating the founding of Princeton's University's Center for Human Values, 1990. First published by Princeton University Press, 1992.)

Thompson, E.P. (1963) *The Making of the English Working Class*. London: Victor Gollancz.

Todorov, T. (2002) *Imperfect Garden: The Legacy of Humanism* (Trans. C. Cosman). Princeton and Oxford: Princeton University Press.

Universities UK (2008) *The Changing Academic Profession in the UK and Beyond*. London: Universities UK.

Vally, S. (2010) Reading Edward Said in South Africa – The Slippery Side of the Academy: From Ivory Tower to Market Mill. Paper Presented at the World Congress for Middle Eastern Studies, Barcelona, Spain, 19–24 July.

Veeser, H.A. (2010) *Edward Said: The Charisma of Criticism*. New York and London: Routledge.

Vico, G. (2001) *New Science: Principles of the New Science Concerning the Common Nature of Nations* (3rd Edition of 1744) (Trans. D. Marsh). London: Penguin Book.

Villa, D. (1996) *Arendt and Heidegger: The Fate of the Political.* Princeton, NJ: Princeton University Press.

— (1999) *Politics, Philosophy, Terror: Essays on the Thought of Hannah Arendt,* Princeton, NJ: Princeton University Press.

— (2001) *Socratic Citizenship.* Princeton and Oxford: Princeton University Press.

— (2008) *Public Freedom.* Princeton and Oxford: Princeton University Press.

Wilby, P. (2011) This half-baked Ivy League spells two tiers of unfairness. *The Guardian* (30 June) p. 35.

Williams, G.L. (1995) The 'marketization' of higher education: reforms and potentials in higher education finance, in D.D. Dill and B. Sporn (eds) *Emerging Patterns of Social Demand and University Reform: Through a Glass Darkly.* Oxford, New York and Tokyo: Pergamon for the International Association of Universities Press.

Williams, R. (1958) *Culture and Society.* London: Chatto and Windus.

— (1961) *The Long Revolution.* London: Chatto and Windus.

Winnicott, D.W. (1965) *The Maturational Process and the Facilitating Environment.* New York: International Universities Press.

— (1986) *Holding and Interpretation: Fragment of an Analysis.* New York: Grove.

Wittgenstein, L. (2001) *Tractatus Logico-Philosophicus* (Trans. D.F. Pears and B.F. McGuinness). London and New York: Routledge. (1st English Edition 1922).

Wolff, J. and De-Shalit, A. (2007) *Disadvantage.* New York: Oxford University Press.

Young, M. (1958) *The Rise of Meritocracy, 1870–2033: An Essay on Education and Equality.* London: Penguin.

Young-Bruehl, E. (1982) *Hannah Arendt: For Love of the World.* New Haven and London: Yale University of Press.

— (2006) *Why Arendt Matters.* New Haven and London: Yale University Press.

Young-Bruehl, E. and Kohn, J. (2001) What and how we learned from Hannah Arendt: an exchange of letters, in M. Gordon (ed) *Hannah Arendt and Education: Renewing Our Common World.* Boulder, Col and Oxford: Westview Press, pp. 225–256.

Index